DESIGNING AND CREATING A
COTTAGE GARDEN

DESIGNING AND CREATING A
COTTAGE GARDEN

HOW TO CULTIVATE A GARDEN FULL OF FLOWERS, HERBS, TREES, FRUIT, VEGETABLES AND LIVESTOCK, WITH 500 INSPIRATIONAL PHOTOGRAPHS

GAIL HARLAND

Special photography by Howard Rice and Steven Wooster

This edition is published by Aquamarine
an imprint of Anness Publishing Ltd

info@anness.com

www.aquamarinebooks.com; www.annesspublishing.com

If you like the images in this book and would like to investigate using
them for publishing, promotions or advertising, please visit our
website www.practicalpictures.com for more information.

© Anness Publishing Ltd 2021

A CIP catalogue record for this book is available from
the British Library.

Publisher: Joanna Lorenz
Project editor: Emma Clegg
Designers: Talking Design
Practical photography and directory shots: Howard Rice
Location photography: Steven Wooster
Production: Ben Worley

PUBLISHER'S NOTES

Although the advice and information in this book are believed
to be accurate and true at the time of going to press, neither the
authors nor the publisher can accept any legal responsibility or liability
for any errors or omissions that may have been made nor for any
inaccuracies nor for any loss, harm or injury that comes about from
following instructions or advice in this book.

Great care should be taken if you include pools, ponds or water features
as part of your garden landscape. Young children should never be left
unsupervised near water of any depth, and if children are able to access
the garden all pools and ponds should be fenced and gated to the
recommended specifications.

In the United States, throughout the Sun Belt states, from Florida,
across the Gulf Coast, south Texas, southern deserts to Southern
California and coastal regions, annuals are planted in the autumn,
bloom in the winter and spring, and die at the beginning of summer.

contents

introduction
The term 'cottage garden' conjures up images of a cheerful profusion of flowers surrounding a thatched cottage, with honeysuckle and roses around the door, and scarlet pelargoniums craning towards the light in tiny windows. Cottage gardens, however, are not exclusively nostalgic, and are just as suited to modern homes as to classic country dwellings. What is more, traditional features of the cottage garden – such as edible plants interwoven with ornamentals, informal mixed plantings and the use of native plants – have universal appeal and are seen in all styles of garden.

ABOVE: *This cottage garden has relaxed planting and a birdbox to house avian visitors.*

RIGHT: *Naked ladies (Nerine) give colour in autumn when summer flowers have faded.*

FAR RIGHT: *Productive cottage gardens can provide figs and other crops for all the family.*

BELOW RIGHT: *Geese are great characters, beside being efficient and ecofriendly lawnmowers.*

OPPOSITE: *Intrinsic to the cottage garden style is a sense of informality and generosity within the planting.*

The cottage garden can be recognized primarily by its adaptability and its informality. It may be a tiny yard or a large, open space with a meadow and orchard, but it can usually be distinguished by an intimate atmosphere, relaxed, sometimes humorous, touches, and a softness in the planting.

Plants are fundamental – indeed, the first cottage gardens were used mainly to produce plants for human consumption and for feeding livestock, as well as for growing strewing herbs, dye plants and plants for medicinal purposes. An ornamental approach was of less importance. With increased wealth and leisure time, the growing of plants for their intrinsic beauty and interest has became more common, but there is always a practical element. Herbs are grown for use as well as to look and smell good, and some space will be found for a strawberry pot, or salad leaves among the flowers.

Having your own cottage garden can be a richly satisfying experience. Moreover, the style can be created in any kind of home and on a limited budget – a make-do ideology was, after all,

integral to the first cottage gardens and the rural population who used them. Reading plant lists from books and magazines, and visiting garden centres may give you ideas, but a true cottage garden is more likely to be full of plants grown from locally sourced cuttings. In the same way, a simple bench made from two logs and a plank of wood is more appropriate and charming than a trendy, expensive store-bought product.

This rustic, practical approach is also a method of keeping things simple in our frenetic modern world, so that the way we manage our gardens is sustainable and in tune with the environment. If you grow at least a proportion of your own food then the advantages are threefold – you save money, reduce the need for long-distance transport and increase the quality of the food on your plate. Even the smallest garden, tub or window box can produce fresh and tasty fruits, herbs or vegetables.

Deciding to keep chickens or ducks will promote a healthy economy in a small garden, while those with more space may decide to keep larger livestock such as goats or pigs. Animals of any kind bring life to the cottage garden, and even with no livestock the rich, dense cottage planting style is attractive to wildlife, and will ensure that your cottage garden patch is a stimulating and animated environment.

the evolution of the cottage garden

A cottage garden is seen by many as a wholly English concept, something of a chocolate-box cliché, a romantic tumble of plants billowing around a pretty cottage in a sleepy country village. There is a wealth of documentation about this style of gardening in the United Kingdom. From Victorian times onward some of the great names of British gardening, such as William Robinson and Margery Fish, championed the style, while artists such as Helen Allingham and Beatrice Parsons immortalized images of country gardens in paint. However, cottage gardens can be seen all over the world, wherever people have a plot of land to grow food for the family. Mixing edible crops with easily available ornamental plants evolves into a relaxed garden that is totally practical and as relevant for the 21st century as it was for the first cottagers.

LEFT: *This idyllic cottage and flower-filled garden near Stratford-upon-Avon, England, dates from the 15th century and was the childhood home of Shakespeare's wife, Anne Hathaway.* ABOVE LEFT: *Wild daffodils such as Narcissus pseudonarcissus are an uplifting addition to any informal or cottage garden.* ABOVE CENTRE: *Self-seeding plants make even workaday areas attractive.* ABOVE RIGHT: *Tulips from Central Asia are now popular cottage garden plants.*

subsistence gardening & estate cottages

The first cottage gardens were created by tenants using land provided by the estate owners on which they could grow their own crops. While life was hard for the cottagers, they were able to grow food and medicines and keep livestock to support their families.

ABOVE: *The cabbage* (Brassica oleracea capitata) *has been grown for more than 4,000 years.*

BELOW: *Harvesting spinach, from* Tacuinum Sanitatis, *a medieval book advising that a healthy life should be lived in harmony.*

BELOW RIGHT: *Spring garden tasks shown by Dutch painter Jacob Grimmer (c.1526–89).*

Subsistence gardening

The earliest cottage gardens in England were created after a devastating outbreak of the Black Death in 1349. The plague killed a third of the population and the resulting shortage of labour obliged landowners to let their land to tenants, creating a class of free labourers who for the first time had their own cottage and plot of land, and a means of growing food for themselves. Commonly grown crops were cabbages, turnips, beans, onions, leeks and herbs. The beans were used to make flour or porridge, while the turnips and cabbages were grown for use in soup-like pottages. Tree fruit such as apples and pears could be stored over the winter. Cherries, red or black currants and English gooseberries were also popular. Raspberries were not grown until the 16th century, when many other garden crops were introduced.

The early cottage gardens of the 14th century probably devoted as much space to keeping livestock as to growing plants. Animals often spent winter nights inside the cottage, providing extra warmth in the days before central heating. Although livestock often grazed on common land, winter fodder for the animals was also grown in the cottage garden.

Urban cottage gardens

Cottage gardens were not restricted to the countryside. In the Middle Ages, town cottages in the suburbs of many European cities had small gardens, where the owner or tenant could grow pot herbs and salad vegetables or a couple of fruit trees. Such gardens, often in the care of skilled craftsmen or guild members, were important to people who no longer had easy access to the wild plants of the fields and hedgerows.

The monastic influence

In the Middle Ages monasteries flourished, and their garden management had an early influence on cottage gardens. In the Carthusian monasteries, each monk had his own garden behind his cell. Medicinal plants were essential, but, for those with time for contemplation, flowers such as peonies (*Paeonia*), primroses (*Primula*) and pinks (*Dianthus*) would have been irresistible. It was in the monastery and physic gardens that the idea arose of segregating different types of plant into separate beds, often surrounded by a border of lavender or box.

Estate cottages

Conditions were harsh for the average cottager for hundreds of years. Sometimes, enlightened landowners tried to improve their tenants' quality of life. In the 1760s, the prison reformer John Howard spent considerable sums of money improving the cottages on his estate in Bedfordshire, England, and providing education for his workers' children. Others supplied common pasture so that tenants could graze their own cattle, or sizeable cottage gardens or allotments on which they could grow food for the family. Not all landowners were so altruistic, of course, and sometimes cottages were swept away for the simple reason that they impeded a view.

In Victorian times, a number of philanthropic schemes were tried to help the poor. A report in the *Gardener's Chronicle* magazine in 1861 described a vegetable exhibition held by The Sudbury Cottagers that encouraged local cottagers to show their produce and receive prizes. Several magazines, including *The Cottage Gardener*, were published to promote developments in horticulture. They were widely read, even by many who could not afford to buy them, as copies would be passed among friends.

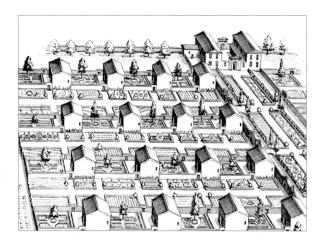

ABOVE: **The Kitchen Garden** *by Bernard de Hoog (1866–1943) shows Victorian cottagers tending their household vegetable garden.*

LEFT: *Garden of a monastery in Turin (engraving) in the early 17th century. The individual small plots allowed monks to grow food crops.*

new plants & how they were introduced

Cottage garden plants were usually native to the region, because they were hardy and available. However, plant-hunting expeditions led to the introduction of many new varieties. The most popular were those that were easy to propagate and so share around.

ABOVE: Fritillaria imperialis *was one of the first cultivated plants.*

BELOW: *Roses, carnations and love-in-a-mist in a painting by Isaak Denies (1647–90).*

BELOW RIGHT: *Josephine Tasher de la Pagerie (1763–1814), Empress of France, with a vase of hydrangeas behind her.*

Informal exchange

The first distinct plant cultivars in the cottage garden were simply natural variants of wild plants, that a cottager might have noticed in the neighbourhood and taken home to grow in his or her garden. There was neither the habit of, nor the money for, investing in new plant specimens, so cottage garden plants became established in a locality by the friendly exchange of clippings and seeds from fruits and vegetables. Because space was precious, many plants were used that could be trained on fences and walls, which left more room for them to spread out. These first cottage gardeners were the rural poor, hard-working folk who used their land as a practical way of providing their families with food. At this stage, growing flowers for prettiness was not a consideration.

The era of exploration

During the 16th and 17th centuries the exploration of new countries and continents meant that new plants from around the world found their way into cottage gardens. The exotic-looking crown imperial (*Fritillaria imperialis*), for example, was introduced from Turkey to Vienna in 1576, where it was grown in the Imperial Gardens. It was mentioned by Shakespeare in his play *The Winter's Tale*, published in 1623, and by that time it was already considered a relatively common plant.

The 17th century, in particular, was a time of great exploration when plants from all parts of the world were sent back for study and cultivation. Many plants from North America, such as the Virginia creeper (*Parthenocissus quinquefolia*) and Virginia stocks (*Malcolmia maritima*), were

introduced to Europe during this period. Another introduction of horticultural interest at this time is the Jerusalem artichoke (*Helianthus tuberosus*). Originally grown in pre-Columbian North America for their edible tubers, Jerusalem artichokes were called potatoes of Canada when they were first introduced to Europe and were considered a great delicacy. By the mid-17th century they had become commonplace.

Jealousy and benevolence

Plant collecting became a competitive business during this period, with botanic gardens and many members of the wealthier classes anxious to show off their latest acquisitions. The collectors endured difficult conditions and hazards in their quest to discover new plants. The Scottish plant collector David Douglas, who undertook a number of expeditions to North America, introduced many cottage-garden favourites to Europe, such as Californian poppies (*Eschscholzia californica*) and the flowering currant (*Ribes sanguineum*).

While most gardeners were generous with their plants, there were notable exceptions. Napoleon's Empress Josephine (1763–1814), for example, was said to have

jealously guarded her collection of dahlias. It is said that a lady-in-waiting bribed one of the gardeners to give her some dahlias, but when she was later heard boasting of the deed Josephine banished the lady, dismissed the gardener and destroyed all the dahlias. Even seemingly altruistic acts could have ulterior motives. In 1829, John Claudius Loudon (1783–1843) recommended that the gardeners of country gentlemen should give showy plants, such as pelargoniums, fuchsias and heliotropes, to the cottagers on their masters' estates for decorating their roadside gardens. But this was intended as much for the benefit of the estate owners and their visitors as for the enjoyment of the cottagers.

The gardeners on some large estates in the Victorian era were genuinely benevolent. Donald Beaton, head gardener at Shrubland Park in Suffolk, England, introduced several pelargoniums. In the 1840s, he wrote for the garden journal *The Cottage Gardener*, in which he recorded that he never sold any of his master's plants because he felt this to be an abuse of his position. However, he would give plants away to anyone who wanted them on condition that they should be returned to him if the recipient did not like the plants.

ABOVE: *A study of crown imperials and lily by Alexander Marshal (c.1625–82) – these exotic flowers became fashionable after their introduction to Europe in the 16th and 17th centuries.*

florists' societies & gooseberry clubs While informality

is the guiding principle of the cottage-garden style, many garden enthusiasts develop an overwhelming interest in one particular group of plants. As a result, well-ordered collections of florists' flowers have become a regular feature of cottage gardens.

ABOVE: *The gold-laced polyanthus was particularly popular in the first half of the 19th century.*

RIGHT: *A painting of an early morning market in 1898 – the evolution of the cottage garden is closely linked to the development and popularization of florist's favourites.*

BELOW RIGHT: *Weighmen at the Egton Bridge Gooseberry Show, near Whitby in the north of England, the only remaining open-admission show.*

Florists' societies

Traditionally grown in the cottage garden were florists' flowers such as primroses and violets. The enthusiasm for specific flowers such as these led to the development of florists' societies around the end of the 18th century.

The word florist in this context means someone who specializes in growing, breeding and exhibiting a particular type of flower. The skills of the florist are generally acknowledged to have been introduced to Britain by Huguenot refugees. Many such immigrants were skilled workers with a great knowledge of the textile industries. Weavers who worked at home all day were in an ideal position to look after specialist plants such as show auriculas, which often have a powdery farina on leaves and flowers that would be washed off if they were exposed to rain.

Florists' societies thrived in towns in the north of England, such as Cheshire, Derbyshire and Yorkshire, where many cottage craftsmen and mill workers lived. Florists in Staffordshire were particularly known for growing polyanthus, and those in Lancashire for cultivating show auriculas (*Primula auricula*). In Paisley, in Scotland, laced pinks were popular with weavers, who used these flowers as design motifs to weave into paisley shawls. At first, a wide range of plants were grown, but by the 18th century only eight groups were deemed worthy of attention: anemones, auriculas, carnations, hyacinths, pinks, polyanthus, ranunculus and tulips. In Victorian times the list of acceptable florists' flowers was expanded to include non-hardy plants, such as dahlias, chrysanthemums and pelargoniums, as well as sweet Williams (*Dianthus barbatus*), pansies (*Viola x wittrockiana*) and hollyhocks (*Alcea rosea*).

Flower shows or florists' feasts were usually held in public houses. The landlord or some other patron would offer prizes such as silver spoons or copper kettles. Flowers were displayed either cut or in their pots. Judging was exacting and the flowers had to follow strict criteria. A meal generally followed the judging and was an important social occasion for those involved. There would be rivalry, friendly or otherwise, between competitors, with some jealously guarding their recipes for special potting mixes and growing methods.

Gooseberry clubs

It was not just flowers that attracted bands of devotees. The gooseberry was also popular with cottage gardeners in the industrial Midlands and the north of England, where the moist climate is particularly conducive to their growth. From the early 19th century, specialist gooseberry clubs held shows with prizes awarded for the heaviest berries. There are classes for different coloured berries but the weight is the most important factor, with the heaviest gooseberry winning the Champion Berry prize. Some cultivars, such as 'London' and 'Woodpecker', can have berries the size of hens' eggs. At one stage, more than 2,000 cultivars were grown, with fruits ranging from the traditional tart berry to meltingly sweet dessert fruit. Show plants were grown in rows inside long pens, low wooden frameworks that supported a net to keep birds off the plants.

As with many florists' flowers, the popularity of growing gooseberries has declined dramatically since its heyday. Of the hundreds of gooseberry clubs once thriving in northern England, only ten now remain, mostly in Cheshire, although the Egton Bridge Old Gooseberry Show in North Yorkshire, whose records go back to 1800, is probably the oldest. The Cheshire Landscape Trust, in association with local schools, is currently trying to maintain the traditions of gooseberry growing in the region.

ABOVE LEFT: *A pedestal vase is arranged with carnations for the British Carnation Society Show, held in London's Royal Horticultural Society Hall (ca. 1925).*

ABOVE: *English tulips at the Wakefield and North of England Tulip Society annual show – traditionally displayed in brown beer bottles.*

the Victorian ideal

In the 19th century, cottage gardens – with their distinctive blend of useful and ornamental plants and the heady rural enchantment of the crowded flowers and home-grown produce – attracted many admirers including writers and artists. Their work may have romanticized the subject, but remains an enduring inspiration.

ABOVE: *The white Madonna lily (Lilium candidum) is a highly fragrant summer-flowering cottage garden favourite.*

BELOW: *The garden of Margery Fish at East Lambrook Manor in Somerset, England, was lovingly described in many of her books including* We Made a Garden *(1956).*

Garden designers and writers

The cottage garden was simply a means of subsistence, until the romantic ideals of the Victorian era brought it to the attention of the middle classes. A rural way of life, the charms of nature in harmony and a profusion of traditional, fragrant flowers were seen as an escape from the harsh realities of the fast-developing industrial world and a way of soothing the spirit. Here are a selection of the writers and designers who helped form this new perspective.

William Robinson (1838–1935)

In *The English Flower Garden* (1883), the gardener William Robinson enthused on the year-round prettiness of the cottage garden, and the rich fragrance of traditional flowers such as Madonna lilies (*Lilium candidum*) and wallflowers (*Cheiranthus cheiri*). His garden at Gravetye Manor in Sussex, England, was painted by popular artists such as Beatrice Parsons (1870–1955) and Henry Moon (1857–1905).

Gertrude Jekyll (1843–1932)

Often regarded as the doyenne of English garden writers, Gertrude Jekyll was a supporter of Robinson's ideas on natural planting. Although most closely associated with extensive, colour-themed flower borders, her books reveal a strong fascination for the cottage-garden style.

Major Lawrence Johnston (1871–1958)

A soldier and garden designer, Johnston created the garden at Hidcote Manor, in Gloucestershire, England. Using a framework of clipped hedges, the garden provides separate areas in which

plants could grow in harmony, with climbers scrambling over hedges, herbaceous plants intermingling with bulbs, old roses in the kitchen garden, and self-seeders spreading as they pleased.

Margery Fish (1888–1969)

The influential writings of Margery Fish are paeans to the simple plants of the cottage garden. She was a powerful advocate of the conservation of old-fashioned flowers, and started a nursery to make such plants more widely available to the public. Her garden at East Lambrook Manor in Somerset, England, is a celebration of the ornamental approach to cottage gardening. Planted with evergreens for year-round structure, the garden also has an exceptional range of other plants, including local wild flowers and cottage-garden favourites.

Vita Sackville-West (1892–1962)

An enthusiast of old-fashioned plants, the cottage-garden 'room' at Vita Sackville-West's garden at Sissinghurst in Kent, England, mixed herbaceous and bulbous plants with roses and shrubs in typical cottage-garden fashion. The section of the garden around the South Cottage was designed as an intimate space with a muddle of flowers and self-seeding specimens. Elsewhere in the large garden she used a less traditional, more contrived colour scheme and exotic plants brought back from her travels.

Christopher Lloyd (1921–2006)

The late writer and gardener, Christopher Lloyd, was perhaps best known for his gardens at Great Dixter in Sussex, England, which demonstrate that an informal cottage-garden style can be appropriate in any setting. Lloyd enjoyed experimenting with plants, which meant that his garden was constantly evolving. Elements of his garden, such as the wild orchids flourishing in the meadows and poppies self-seeding in cracks in the paving, are much imitated.

Geoff Hamilton (1936–1996)

The gardener and broadcaster Geoff Hamilton did much to bring cottage gardening to the public's notice. His television series *Geoff Hamilton's Cottage Gardens* had a down-to-earth appeal, showing Hamilton creating two cottage gardens, an "artisan's garden" using low-cost materials, and a no-expense-spared "gentleman's garden". He was president of the Cottage Garden Society and a strong champion of gardening without chemicals.

Artists' gardens

Admiration for the cottage garden was not confined to a few garden writers. The idealized country scenes of 19th- and 20th-century painters such as Myles Birket Foster (1825–1899) and Helen Allingham (1848–1926), showing the cottage garden as an idyll inhabited by contented people, were extremely popular. In an increasingly industrial age, romantic notions of a life of rural simplicity held a great attraction, and the traditional cottage garden was seen as a retreat akin to the flowery meadow of medieval times. Later, in England, the artist Sir Cedric Morris (1889–1982) created a garden surrounding his 16th-century house at Benton End in Suffolk. The garden, which was used to raise vegetables and a jumble of flowers, featured in many of his paintings.

ABOVE: *English poet and novelist Vita Sackville-West (1892–1962) in her garden at Sissinghurst, Kent, c. 1960.*

LEFT: **In Munstead Wood Garden** *is a watercolour by Helen Allingham (1848–1926) showing Gertrude Jekyll's garden in Godalming, Surrey, England.*

taking inspiration from around the world

Cottage gardens have universal appeal and there are various international gardens, notably in North America and Europe, that offer planting ideas or interpretations of the style. The everyday examples here show how recognizable the themes are despite climatic variations.

TOP: *Fig trees provide fruit and shade in Mediterranean gardens and were widely planted in California for the same reasons.*

RIGHT: *A garden at the Historic Mission San Juan Capistrano in Orange County, California.*

BELOW: *A white picket fence with roses,* Centranthus ruber *and alliums, Northern California, USA.*

Notable American gardens

In North America, the first permanent settlements by Europeans were made in Virginia in 1607. The Native Americans already grew their own crops and the settlers soon began to form enclosures and cultivate useful plants. These pioneer gardeners grew beans, cabbages and corn, but also flowers such as roses, hollyhocks (*Alcea rosea*) and peonies (*Paeonia*) that reminded them of their homeland.

The Mount Vernon estate, which George Washington inherited in 1761, is hardly a cottage garden, but holds records that show which plants were grown. Dwarf box (*Buxus sempervirens* 'Suffruticosa') was used to form low borders and parterres, while the kitchen garden contained vegetables, such as beetroot (beets), beans, peas, spinach and onions, and flowers such as larkspur (*Consolida ajacis*), foxgloves (*Digitalis*), crown imperials (*Fritillaria imperialis*) and jasmine. The gardens at Monticello, created by Thomas Jefferson from the late 18th century, were used as a botanical laboratory in which he grew 170 kinds of fruit, as well as favourite flowers like cleomes, hollyhocks and the golden rain tree (*Koelreuteria paniculata*).

In California in the late 19th century, nostalgia for Spanish-style gardens led to popular plantings of climbing roses, vines, and fruit such as figs and pomegranates. Many of the Californian mission gardens contained productive plants such as olive trees (*Olea europaea*), grapevines (*Vitis vinifera*) and orange trees (*Citrus sinensis*), as well as ornamental plants like scented oleanders (*Nerium oleander*). An appreciation of the native flora and the difficulty of creating European-style gardens in a dry climate meant that Californian native species like ceanothus and matilija poppies (*Romneya coulteri*) were also used, as well as plants from Australia such as eucalyptus and bottlebrush (*Callistemon*). Slightly later, the author George Washington Cable (1844–1925) encouraged the planting of old-fashioned gardens with perennials and native flowering

shrubs, surrounded by vine-covered fences, while Tasha Tudor's Vermont garden was an inspiration to many, with its combination of traditional flowers with fruit, vegetables and livestock. Tudor (1915–2008), an author and illustrator, lived very simply, making her own clothes and working barefoot.

Famous European gardens

In Europe, particularly in France and Luxembourg, priests' gardens were another source of inspiration. They possessed seven essential ingredients to fulfil bodily and spiritual needs: fruit and vegetables for the house, a fountain or well, medicinal plants, vines to make wine for mass, flowers to decorate the church, box plants (a symbol of eternity), and a statue of the Virgin Mary. Today, a recreation of a priest's garden can be seen at Viels-Maisons near Paris. Designed by Bertraude de Ladoucette to attract visitors to the adjoining 12th-century Romanesque church, the beds are filled with a profusion of lavender, thyme, box and roses such as 'Lonette Chenault', 'Vent d'Été' and 'Buff Beauty'.

Many artists have used cottage gardens as a subject and some have created their own gardens. Claude Monet's garden at Giverny in France, for example, provided rich and varied

garden subjects for his masterful Impressionist paintings, and the garden has attracted many enthusiasts since the late 19th century. The average cottage garden may not have room for a lake like the one at Giverny, full of waterlilies and bridges dripping with wisteria, but the rich, resonant blocks of garden colour that melt into each other can be achieved anywhere. Giverny's dense, informal plantings of peonies, irises and poppies proved irresistible to painters.

An exhibition of Impressionist paintings in 1886 inspired many American painters, such as John Leslie Breck and Robert Vonnoh, to study the style in France. Some went home to create similar gardens themselves – for example, Gaines Ruger Donoho's garden in East Hampton contained box-edged beds filled with anemones, irises and lilies.

ABOVE LEFT: *A cottage flower garden with rocking chairs in Georgetown, Indiana.*

ABOVE: *Monet's garden at Giverny has romantic swathes of flowers as well as areas devoted to vegetables.*

FAR LEFT: *A traditional country cottage in Funen, Denmark.*

working garden traditions

The cottage garden began as a place in which the cottager grew produce to support his family. As a result there is a cross-pollination of ideas between cottage gardens and other working gardens, all of which aim to make good use of the land available.

ABOVE: *Allotments have always been a place where generations meet, sharing time in a natural setting.*

BELOW: *Allotments are often found in densely populated areas, and give residents a direct connection to the land.*

BELOW RIGHT: *Local residents help in the Dig For Victory allotments at Dulwich, south London, in 1917.*

Shared gardens

There are various types of shared garden, each one connected to the community and self-sufficient ethic of the cottage garden. In the UK and the rest of Europe, allotments are characterized by collections of individual plots. In North America, there are various forms of 'community gardens'. These include small plots as well as 'greening projects', which transform manmade communal areas into green spaces that can be used for growing vegetables, keeping livestock or as pleasant recreation zones.

Allotments

Particularly widely used in Britain, allotments are small parcels of land rented to individuals, usually for the growing of food crops. The size of land varies but is commonly ten rods, an ancient measurement roughly equivalent to 250 square metres (2691 square feet). Most allotment land is owned by local government bodies or the Church of England.

The idea of allotments originated in the late 16th century when common lands available to all for grazing their animals, collecting firewood and growing food began to be enclosed, thereby dispossessing the poor. In compensation, individuals within communities were provided with areas of land by landowners that they could use for growing their own food.

The General Enclosure Act of 1845 attempted to provide 'field gardens' of a quarter of an acre for the landless poor – this process of enclosure in England was adopted in a similar way in other parts of Europe. While this increased efficiency in agriculture and food supply to the burgeoning urban centres, only a minority benefited; the majority were forced to seek work in the growing urban centres as they lost access to the land. In response to this, certain influential members of the ruling elite of the time enabled the provision of land in the form of allotments, principally for the poor and unemployed, so that they could grow their own produce.

While most allotments are still used for growing vegetables, many also have fruit bushes or trees and flowers. At some sites the keeping of livestock such as chickens is permitted. There is frequently a great camaraderie between gardeners on the site, and the sharing of knowledge and resources makes working an allotment a social, as well as a mutually beneficial, activity. In keeping with cottage gardeners of old, those with allotments often display ingenuity and imagination when raising crops using limited resources. Tumbledown potting sheds or quirky details, such as scarecrows, also give a sense of individuality to plots.

Victory gardens

During the Second World War, food imports to Britain were often intercepted by the enemy, and there was a strong movement to increase food production at home. 'Land girls' replaced male agricultural workers who had gone to fight, and everyone who had access to a garden or allotment was encouraged to grow food. Allotment numbers peaked at around 1,400,000 during the Second World War as a result of the 'Dig for Victory' campaign. This led to the creation of numerous victory or liberty gardens, including a much publicized one in Hyde Park, London. In the US, President Roosevelt called for Americans to grow more vegetables and Eleanor Roosevelt created a victory garden in the White House grounds. The Fenway Victory Gardens in Boston, Massachusetts, established in 1942, still exist.

There is now a new 'Grow your own' movement to lessen reliance on mass-produced or imported food, decrease our carbon footprint, survive difficult economic times and foster a sense of community. While this movement has political aspects, it also echoes the cottage garden ethos of a garden that will feed the soul as well as the body.

Community gardens

Closely related to allotments are community gardens, especially prevalent in the United States, Canada, Australia and New Zealand, in which land is gardened by a group of people. They usually develop when local residents join together to clear abandoned vacant lots and turn them into gardens. Each garden responds to the needs of the community. Land may be used as recreational green space, for food production or for a combination of purposes. Active gardens promote a strong sense of community and have been shown to reduce levels of crime and vandalism. There are estimated to be around 100,000 community gardens in the United States, with more than 1,000 in New York State. In Australia, the first community garden was set up in Nunawading by Dr Gavan Oakley, who saw it as a way of providing occupation and inspiration for both young and elderly people. The Australian Community Gardens Network, started in 1996, helps to promote these gardens and provides practical information to gardeners.

The style of these gardens tends to be informal and relaxed, with both flowers and food crops grown. Seeds and young plants are shared between the community, much in the same way that the cottagers of old would share slips of plants with their neighbours over the garden fence.

ABOVE LEFT: *Leeks, beetroot and parsnips in a community garden in Cambridgeshire, England.*

ABOVE: *Gardeners chatting in a community garden in the Fort Mason Marina District, San Francisco, California.*

styles & seasons

A typical cottage garden would have evolved to suit the available space and the people using it. A traditional and practical approach was to have a straight path between the gate and the front door, beds each side of the path and a bench near the door. Contemporary cottage gardens still need to work around the people that live there, but will also be chosen to harmonize with the style of home. This chapter introduces seven style ideas for the cottage garden, including a productive garden that cultivates vegetables, fruit and herbs, a courtyard garden for a smaller, container-filled hard-landscaped area, and a 'secret' garden with sheltering trees, nooks and shadows. Whichever style you prefer, think hard about making the garden work all year round. This chapter finishes with a selection of ideas for each garden season to ensure that the garden is a delight at every stage of the year – just as the first cottagers would have done.

LEFT: *Richly coloured lilies and roses in this front garden echo the colour of the main door.* ABOVE LEFT: *Early spring flowers, such as this damson blossom, lift the spirits at the start of the year.* ABOVE CENTRE: Cyclamen hederifolium *is an easy-to-grow plant with dainty autumn flowers.* ABOVE RIGHT: *Frosted winter buds such as these hold the promise of flowers to come.*

the flowery bower
The early cottagers would not have had the time for relaxation, but arbours and flowery bowers, formed by training plants such as honeysuckle (*Lonicera*) and morning glory (*Ipomoea*) over a natural or manmade framework, are romantic features that fit beautifully within a cottage garden.

ABOVE: *Honeysuckle (Lonicera x italica) has wonderfully fragrant flowers.*

BELOW LEFT: *This living willow arbour with an internal grass seat provides an attractive garden refuge.*

BELOW CENTRE: *Rustic arbours create secluded seating areas within the garden.*

BELOW RIGHT: *Rambling roses entwine with honeysuckle and a climbing vine to give a sense of wild profusion.*

OPPOSITE: *Clematis and roses climbing over a wooden arched structure create a magical combination of perfume and summer colour.*

Living canopies
If you have a mature tree or dense, evergreen hedge in your garden, you may be able to turn it into a bower. Remove any large, forward-facing branches, and trim and train the others to create a living canopy under which you can put a bench. Alternatively, you can plant a tree and train it to the required shape as it grows. Obviously, this approach requires time and patience, but it does give the opportunity to train low-growing branches to form a seat under the canopy.

Choosing a tree with a weeping habit will make subsequent training easier. You could try the beautiful, silver-leafed pear, *Pyrus salicifolia* 'Pendula', the medlar, *Mespilus germanica* 'Large Russian', or the weeping white mulberry, *Morus alba* 'Pendula'. If plenty of space is available, consider the weeping ash, *Fraxinus excelsior* 'Pendula', or the weeping silver lime, *Tilia* 'Petiolaris'. *T.* 'Petiolaris' has highly scented flowers and is not susceptible to the aphid problems of the common lime, but will reach 30m (100ft) if it is not pruned. A weeping crab apple such as *Malus x scheideckeri* 'Red Jade' or *M. x gloriosa* 'Oekonomierat Echtermeyer' will make a less dense canopy, but will provide a brilliant display of blossom followed by colourful fruits.

Trailing flowers
Once the tree or hedge has grown large enough to accommodate a bench, start to cover it with flowers. Vigorous climbers, such as many honeysuckles, may overwhelm a young tree, so be cautious at first and use some of the less rampant annual climbers such as sweet peas (*Lathyrus odoratus*) and the purple bell vine *Rhodochiton atrosanguineum*. Plant them towards the outer edge of the tree canopy so that they are not competing with the tree for water and nutrients. If the branches do not come down low enough, the climbers may initially need a bamboo cane for support. *Lophospermum erubescens*, black-eyed Susan (*Thunbergia alata*) and the canary creeper (*Tropaeolum peregrinum*) will quickly cover the bower with cheerful flowers. For the ultimate in romance, plant the moonflower (*Ipomoea alba*), which in hot summers will produce a steady supply of pure white, highly fragrant trumpets that open in the evening.

Willow arbours
As an alternative to a tree bower, you could make a living willow arbour. A semi-circle of cut willow stems inserted into prepared ground over the autumn or winter months usually roots quickly and can be woven to form a green canopy over which you can train fast-growing annuals such as morning glories (*Ipomoea*) or sweet peas in its first summer. Willow (*Salix*) is an ideal material for creating natural-looking fencing and for weaving work. You will need shorter lengths for fine-quality weaving and longer ones for fencing.

The view from the bower should encourage you to linger there. Plant a profusion of pretty, scented flowers nearby or use flower containers so that they can be changed as they bloom and fade. Pots of edible plants such as a dessert grapevine, cherry tomatoes or strawberries will give you something to nibble while sitting in your bower. If the bower is screened in some way, it can also be a trysting space.

the scented garden

Roses, lilacs, lavenders and heliotrope are just some of the fragrant plants that heighten the cottage garden experience. There are other perfumed options apart from flowers. Plants such as herbs and scented pelargoniums have aromatic leaves, while the refreshing scent of cut grass forms part of the delight of summer.

Ground-level scents

Start at your feet when creating a scented garden by planting creeping herbs such as thyme (*Thymus*) in paving stone cracks or by laying a chamomile lawn (using the non-flowering *Chamaemelum nobile* 'Treneague'). Line garden paths with lavenders (*Lavandula*) and other aromatic plants so that their scent is released as visitors brush past. Shrubs such as philadelphus and viburnums will release their perfume at head height, while you can also have fragrance in the air by planting climbers like jasmines (*Jasminum*) and honeysuckles (*Lonicera*).

Seasonal options

The first fragrant plants of the year will be early violets (*Viola*) and honey-scented snowdrops (*Galanthus*), as well as other spring bulbs such as the wild jonquil (*Narcissus jonquilla*). *Cytisus battandieri* fills the summer air with a pineapple scent, while *Heliotropium arborescens* cultivars have the perfume of cherry pie.

Scent can vary within a genus. The bearded irises of early summer have perfumes that can be described as sweet, fruity, rose-like, peppery or even like pure chocolate in cultivars such as 'Dusky Challenger'. Summer's profusion includes the ever-popular roses (*Rosa*) and lilies (*Lilium*), giving way to autumn-flowering shrubs such as *Elaeagnus x ebbingei* and *Osmanthus heterophyllus*. The coconut-scented blooms of the double-flowered gorse (*Ulex europaeus* 'Flore Pleno') are produced intermittently throughout the year. Winter scents can be some of the richest of all and no garden should be without daphnes, *Lonicera x purpusii* 'Winter Beauty' and the Algerian iris, *Iris unguicularis*.

Key situations

Don't overload one area of the garden with too many scents, as then the impact of individual fragrances may be lost. Focus on areas where fragrance would best be appreciated – by the garden gate or front door, for example. Seating areas are also excellent places to plant fragrant species, scented pelargoniums being particularly useful beside a bench because you can sit and rub their leaves to enjoy the aroma.

Some plants only release their perfume at specific times. The aromatic oils in many herbs are concentrated during the heat of the day and so the scents tend to be most noticeable on sunny afternoons. Planting these species in sunny, sheltered corners where they can bask in the additional heat stored by walls and paving will help to intensify the fragrance.

In the evening, night-scented flowers add a different dimension to the garden. The night-scented stock (*Matthiola longipetala* subsp. *bicornis*) is one of the easiest plants to grow, with modest, pink or lilac flowers that can look rather undistinguished during the day. At sunset, however, the flowers open wide, releasing a strong, spicy perfume with hints of vanilla and clove. Scatter the seed in spring beneath a window to enjoy the perfume on warm summer evenings. The other cottage-garden classic for night scent is the evening primrose (*Oenothera biennis*), a tall annual or biennial plant whose flowers open pale yellow and age to pure gold. A more recent introduction is *Zaluzianskya ovata*, which is best grown in a pot in cold areas. The red-backed, white flowers open in the evening to produce an intoxicating scent.

ABOVE: *Bearded irises are noted for their strong fragrance, which ranges from subtle and light to deep and sugary.*

BELOW LEFT: *Snowdrops (*Galanthus nivalis*) have a honey fragrance, especially clear on still, sunny days.*

BELOW CENTRE: *Brushing past the plants in this thyme pavement releases their spicy scent.*

BELOW RIGHT: Heliotropium arborescens *is loved for its distinctive cherry-pie fragrance.*

OPPOSITE: *This chaotic profusion of summer roses welcomes visitors to the garden.*

the herb garden

As plants used for culinary or medicinal purposes, herbs had a central role in the productive cottage garden. Today's herb gardens contain both useful and ornamental plants – they might feature catmint for a warming tea, curry plant to add to soups or stews, hyssop for a path edging or borage for attracting butterflies.

ABOVE: *Chives are a useful culinary herb and the flowers attract bees.*

BELOW LEFT: *Purple and green-leaved sage are ideal plants for the front of a herb border.*

BELOW CENTRE: *Thyme grown in a strawberry pot makes an attractive feature in a herb garden, especially combined with a contrasting background.*

BELOW RIGHT: *Box and cotton lavender can be grown together to give contrasting foliage.*

OPPOSITE: *Lavender, fennel, tricoloured sage and parsley form a colourful bed, with vegetables, strawberries and flowers.*

Site preferences

Most herbs prefer a sunny site and well-drained soil. Don't, however, dismiss the idea of a herb garden if your garden doesn't provide these conditions, because plants such as common chervil (*Anthriscus cerefolium*), chives (*Allium schoenoprasum*), sweet Cicely (*Myrrhis odorata*) and many mints (*Mentha*) will grow in moist shade. Provide shelter to protect herbs, if necessary, and ensure that their fragrance is not carried away with the wind. Trellis screens or rosemary hedging both look appropriate around a herb garden.

Bed definition and access

Herb beds are traditionally edged with hedges of dwarf box (*Buxus sempervirens* 'Suffruticosa'). These do require careful trimming and can compete for water and nutrients. Timber boards, woven willow edgings, old roofing tiles or low brick walls all make suitable bed edgings. Beds raised clear of pathways are particularly helpful on poorly drained sites. They also make it easier to tend to the herbs and can be enhanced with nasturtiums (*Tropaeolum majus*) spilling over the edges.

Herb gardens need firm paths that won't deteriorate into a muddy mess in winter. Brick paths are hardwearing and charming, particularly when laid in a herringbone or basketweave pattern. If you have cold winters, try to get frost-resistant bricks to prevent them flaking. Gravel or pea-shingle paths look effective in Mediterranean-style herb gardens. Laying the gravel over a weed-suppressing membrane prevents prolific self-seeders such as fennel (*Foeniculum vulgare*) taking over.

Making your herb selections

Choosing which herb varieties to grow is one of the most exciting parts of creating a herb garden. Start with those herbs that you use regularly in the kitchen. Think, too, about their ornamental appeal. Many herbs have pleasing coloured-leaved forms. One example is the rich colours of purple sage (*Salvia officinalis* Purpurascens Group), which creates harmonious colour blends with plants such as old-fashioned pinks (*Dianthus*), and has leaves that are as strongly flavoured as the usual form. Indeed, plants such as pinks that have edible flowers are another good addition to the herb garden. Though most are best used sparingly, edible flowers can make a salad look wonderful. Try using *Dianthus* 'Sops-in-wine', violets (*Viola*), nasturtiums, petals of pot marigolds (*Calendula officinalis*) and borage (*Borago officinalis*).

Many herbs can be grown in containers. As well as flowerpots, there are troughs, urns, old sinks, chimney pots and strawberry planters. Using a loam-based potting mix with added grit usually gives the most satisfactory results. A number of herbs such as thyme (*Thymus*), pot marjoram (*Origanum onites*) and creeping rosemary (*Rosmarinus officinalis* Prostratus Group) also work well, grown in window boxes or hanging baskets where they are easy to harvest. They can look very ornamental when combined with cascading tomatoes or chilli peppers. Growing slightly tender herbs such as scented pelargoniums and lemon verbena (*Aloysia triphylla*) in pots means that they can easily be brought under cover for winter.

the productive garden
Productivity was fundamental to the original definition of the cottage garden. The cottagers had to provide food and other essentials for their families. So, while flower gardens have an endless power to enchant and beguile, fruit and vegetable produce enabled self-sufficiency and life-giving provisions.

Size and location

Productive gardens do not need to be large plots. Some crops can be produced in a surprisingly small space and even a window box will supply a decent crop of tomatoes or strawberries. A separate vegetable garden is by no means essential – lettuce may flourish among the flowers and gooseberries can be trained as cordons along a house wall. If you need to maximize the potential crop for economic reasons, however, it is advisable to devote a specific area to growing produce.

Choose a sunny site, preferably away from hedges or overhanging trees that will compete with your crops for water and nutrients. Provide shelter from the wind with a trellis screen or similar and, most importantly, ensure that there is protection from wildlife. It is heartbreaking to raise a promising crop only to find it eaten by deer or rabbits. If you want to grow quantities of soft fruit, such as currants, raspberries and strawberries, then do invest in a fruit cage.

Division and rotation

You will need to divide your plot into at least four areas, so that you can rotate the crops every year. This will help reduce the build-up of plant pests and diseases. If you intend to keep chickens, incorporate their run as part of a rotation scheme so that they will be able to weed and fertilize one plot while you are using others to grow crops. Pigs make useful allies for the initial preparation of the ground, but require sturdy fencing if they are to remain where you want them.

Practicalites

Ensure that paths are wide enough to accommodate a wheelbarrow and firm enough for winter use. Restricting beds to a maximum width of 1.2m (4ft) will allow you to weed and tend to the plants without treading on the bed, which can damage the soil structure. Raised beds are useful because they allow for a greater depth of fertile soil and help to improve drainage. Low-trained fruit trees, sometimes called "step-over" trees, can be used to edge the beds.

Make full use of any walls and fences to grow a range of fruit, which will benefit from the shelter provided and any additional heat stored in the wall. A warm, sunny wall allows you to grow plants, such as apricots, peaches and nectarines, which might normally be considered too tender for your region. If you are able to provide a favourable microclimate in a sheltered part of the garden then you have the opportunity to experiment with less hardy plants.

Essential features such as the compost heap and potting shed should be easily accessible. The potting shed could be painted to blend with its surroundings, and a trellis attached to support climbing plants such as French or runner (green) beans. If you want to start off seeds early in the season or grow tender crops, then it is advisable to use a cold frame or glasshouse. These structures should be situated in an open, sunny site away from children's play areas. Include a bench as part of your design; one that doubles as a tool store is useful, but the crucial factor is that you have somewhere to sit and enjoy the fruits of your labours.

ABOVE: *Swiss chard is a very hardy vegetable and its bright foliage is attractive even in frosty weather.*

BELOW LEFT: *Cabbages and broad (fava) beans are traditional cottage garden crops that are easy to grow.*

BELOW CENTRE: *Cherry tomatoes are highly productive crops for the cottage garden.*

BELOW RIGHT: *These raised beds hold spring onions, sweetcorn, lettuce, cabbages, beetroot and lettuce.*

OPPOSITE: *This productive area of the garden includes crops such as runner beans and courgette (zucchini).*

the courtyard garden

While a courtyard may sound too grand for a cottage garden, an enclosed yard was a regular feature in the working gardens of old, being particularly useful for keeping livestock. Today, however, courtyards are more generally used as an outdoor room, providing a tranquil place to sit and relax or to entertain friends.

ABOVE: *Wisteria is a much-loved trailing plant, a romantic choice for walls, archways, arbours and pergolas.*

BELOW LEFT: *Brick paving makes a lovely warm-coloured foil for mixed plantings.*

BELOW CENTRE: *In this front garden brick setts are used as a robust, hard-wearing paving.*

BELOW RIGHT: *A display of watering cans makes a nostalgic ornamental feature in a corner of this garden.*

OPPOSITE: *Ornaments and metalwork provide textures to offset a soft planting scheme with pink roses and white petunias.*

Hard landscaping

If you need to reassess the floor of your courtyard then local materials will be preferable because they are easier to source, more economical and look more appropriate in the setting. Cobbles create a traditional, cottage-garden ambience, although they are not to everyone's taste as they can be difficult to walk on. Other cottage-style options include bricks, setts, paving slabs and even concrete. The hard landscaping tends to be the most expensive component of a garden design, so if you need to start from scratch, keep it simple and preferably follow the authentic cottage-garden mantra of "make do with what is there".

Partitions and structures

Cottage gardeners would make maximum use of the available space, including using climbing vines and trailing plants on the fences and walls surrounding their garden. Do the same in the modern cottage courtyard to help soften any harsh boundary outlines. In further homage to this approach you can use a screen or trellis planted with decorative or fruiting vines – this will also give an open patio the feeling of an enclosed cottage courtyard. Even a row of shrubs or bamboos in pots will provide a visual screen, giving more of a sense of seclusion.

Erect a pergola or arbour as a sturdy frame for plants such as grape vines (*Vitis vinifera*) and wisteria. This will make the garden more private and create welcome areas of shade in sunny climates. Adding sturdy brackets to the walls also allows for the use of hanging baskets,

Ornament and salvage

Cottage gardens often feature a playful piece of topiary – perhaps a chicken clipped from box (*Buxus*), adding a touch of humour – and these can be planted in pots for the courtyard garden. Using architectural or agricultural salvage items, such as planters, chimney pots or pig-feeding troughs, gives historical character. Use these containers in a sunny courtyard or patio to grow fruit and vegetables, particularly those vegetables such as aubergines (eggplants) and chilli peppers which can benefit from the extra warmth of such situations. Other items of memorabilia such as tin baths, mangles and washboards add interest, as do terracotta plaques or enamel advertising signs on the walls. Take care, however, not to overdo such items, or the garden will lose its restful nature and end up looking a mess.

Furniture

The courtyard garden needs to be a comfortable place in which to relax. To achieve a cottage styling, stone seats are strong and classic choices, and retain summer heat long into the evening. However, they are cold to sit on in winter, and are uncomfortable without cushions.

Metal is another popular material for garden furniture, and wrought iron in traditional designs can be very attractive. However, it can get too hot if it is in direct sun for any length of time and will be cold in winter. The best choice for comfort is furniture made of wood, a natural and traditional material with rustic associations which never looks out of place in a cottage garden.

the secret garden

Perhaps we cannot all create the walled garden, heavy with the scent of roses, made famous in Frances Hodgson-Burnett's book, *The Secret Garden*. But, even in a small cottage garden, it is possible to create a sanctuary to which you can retreat, the crucial element being a sense of privacy and seclusion.

Creating a framework

Long, narrow gardens lend themselves to the creation of a secret garden at the bottom of the plot. However, you can create a hidden area in almost any shape or style of garden with the considered use of partitions or screening plants. Having an obvious door or gate into the garden will draw attention to your secret space, so you may want to be more circumspect. Erect fencing, trellis or screens, or plant hedging across your garden to section off the secret garden, but, rather than having one solid barrier, build it in two halves, with one half about 60cm (2ft) or more in front of the other, and slightly overlapping it. A casual onlooker will see the barrier as a solid fence and assume it marks the end of the garden.

Curving paths through the garden will make it seem larger, while tall perennials or shrubs planted on the curve of a path will prevent you seeing what is around the corner, thereby increasing the sense of mystery.

Animating the space

There are many ways to bring your garden to life – garden mobiles or dream-catchers create sound and movement and will help build a mystical atmosphere. If there is room, suspend a swing from a tree bough or hang a hammock from two trees or robust posts, creating a perfect place for leisurely contemplation.

Encourage local birds to fill your garden with song by providing a birdbath, nesting boxes and feeders. Plenty of bushy shrubs will give cover, while plants such as cotoneaster and tree purslane (*Atriplex halimus*) will produce useful seeds and berries. Position bird feeders in an open part of the site, so that predators cannot lurk in ambush.

Magical plants for your hideaway

Most scented plants do best in a sunny site, so if you have a sunny corner, plant pinks (*Dianthus*) or herbs such as lavender (*Lavandula*), which is believed to aid relaxation. Roses are also a must for their scent, but if it is shady, the gallicas, damasks and albas are the most satisfactory. R. 'Alba Maxima', for example, is a great survivor under less-than-perfect conditions and has fragrant flowers that blush on opening, then fade to creamy white. 'Tuscany', a Gallica rose, is a spreading bush with deep maroon-crimson petals and a rich scent. Honeysuckle is also happy in semi-shade.

A secret garden is the perfect place to include a rare and lovely plant. A collection of special snowdrops (*Galanthus*) would be appropriate or, in warm climates, the moonflower (*Ipomoea alba*), which demands a candlelit pilgrimage in the dead of night. The Chilean bellflower (*Lapageria rosea*) is a beautiful climber with flowers that look as if they have been carved out of wax. Plants of the shrubby peony, *P. rockii*, are often very expensive to buy, but are easy (albeit slow) to grow from seed.

Planting a boundary of large-leaved evergreen shrubs can help to muffle external noise. Consider using *Osmanthus × fortunei*, *Eleagnus × ebbingei*, the common laurel (*Prunus laurocerasus*) or, on acid soils, rhododendrons or camellias.

ABOVE: *'Duchesse de Montebello' is a Gallica rose with a strong, sweet fragrance.*

BELOW LEFT: *A secret garden will look more romantic if it is not too manicured.*

BELOW CENTRE: *A hidden garden glimpsed through an opening excites the imagination and draws the viewer in.*

BELOW RIGHT: *Seats positioned on a camomile lawn create a peaceful corner.*

OPPOSITE: *An abundance of climbing plants screens this corner of the garden, giving an air of seclusion and privacy.*

the meadow garden

True wild flower meadows used for their hay crops may be rapidly declining, but the idea of drifts of rustling grasses studded with flowers such as butterfly weed, asters and coneflowers has a nostalgic appeal, and is a perfect feature for a cottage garden. A meadow will also attract insects and birds.

ABOVE: *Hawthorn (Crataegus) provides useful food for winter migrant birds.*

BELOW LEFT: *Ornamental grasses give extra impact to a meadow-style planting.*

BELOW CENTRE: *Tall spuria-type irises are robust enough to compete with grasses in a meadow.*

BELOW RIGHT: *When left to themselves colourful mixtures of annual flowers form self-seeding colonies.*

OPPOSITE: *Ox-eye daisies and lady's mantle (Alchemilla mollis) are typical grassland plants that are easy to grow.*

Ideal meadow conditions

An open, sunny site is most suitable for a meadow garden, preferably on a soil low in fertility. This favours the growth of wild flowers over coarse grasses. If the site is existing grassland, the soil fertility can be reduced by regularly mowing and removing the clippings for a season or two. The desired wild flower species can then be introduced as pot-grown plants by removing cores of turf with a trowel or bulb planter and inserting the plants.

Establishing a meadow

Start by eliminating any vigorous perennial weeds such as docks (*Rumex*) and creeping thistle (*Cirsium arvense*). In bare soil, you will need to establish both the grasses and the wild flowers. You can start with seed, plants or a mixture of both.

Seed should be sown in autumn or spring on to a well-cultivated soil. Where possible, use grass species that are native to the area as they are more likely to thrive. Mixtures of fine grasses and typical meadow flowers are available to suit many soil types. For the first year, the grass should be kept to a height of at least 5–8cm (2–3in) to enable it to build up a good root system. Subsequent management will depend on your site and the flowering times of the species you want to establish. Aim to cut at least two or three times a year, removing the clippings after each cut to prevent the fertility levels rising.

A mixture of plant species will give the longest flowering display and provide a useful source of nectar to encourage bees and butterflies into your garden. Start with early daffodils (*Narcissus*) and progress through a range of summer flowers to the autumn-flowering meadow saffron (*Colchicum autumnale*). You don't have to restrict yourself to native species; you can also include drifts of blue Siberian irises (*Iris sibirica*), bright tulips (*Tulipa*) and Oriental poppies (*Papaver orientale*). Cutting areas of grass at different heights will increase the diversity of species visiting the meadow.

Complementary elements

If your meadow area is large enough, include a few trees or shrubs. If you are introducing grazing animals, they will appreciate the shade, but will also browse the trees unless you protect them. Hawthorns (*Crataegus*) are ideal, with pretty spring blossom followed by haws that birds adore. If you want fruit for eating, then choose apples, pears, quince or medlars, but don't expect big crops from young trees competing with grass.

A tree seat provides a place to enjoy the view, or you could create a willow arbour in a corner. Natural-looking ponds in low-lying areas will also attract a greater range of wildlife.

Mixed-species hedges are the most traditional boundaries for a meadow garden. Native species are preferable for attracting local wildlife, although you can also add plants such as cotoneasters, which have useful berries for birds. Alternatively, willow and hazel hurdles look attractive, although they do not last long. If you want to use the meadow for animals, incorporate stock-proof fencing or a good, dense, well-laid hedge. Don't overstock the land or your dream meadow will lack flowers and consist of unappealing species such as nettles.

the cottage garden in spring
Everyone has their own way of hailing the arrival of spring: to some it is a migrant bird returning, perhaps the first swallow swooping over a pond or a cuckoo in the woods. For others, it is the re-emergence of a favourite plant, a primrose, maybe, or the first daffodil of the year.

ABOVE: *Crocus 'Ard Schenk' can form large colonies of beautiful pure white flowers if they are divided every couple of years.*

BELOW LEFT: *This cottage garden uses tulips to add height and vibrant colour to a spring display.*

BELOW RIGHT: *Hanging baskets should not be restricted to summer use as this colourful spring planting, including cowslips (Bellis) and violas, demonstrates.*

Spring bulbs
It is perhaps flowering bulbs that most sum up the season of spring. Bulbs such as cottage tulips (*Tulipa*) can be used as cheerful temporary fillers to bring splashes of colour to flower beds. Grape hyacinths (*Muscari*) look spectacular when used to create rivers or pools of deep blue. Try growing *M. aucheri* 'Ocean Magic' the flowers of which are a lighter blue than other grape hyacinths and are surmounted by a little white topknot. They associate well with some of the smaller daffodils such as the fragrant, creamy white *Narcissus* 'Thalia' or white *N.* 'Jack Snipe', with its buttercup-yellow trumpet.

Bulbs, however, are at their best when allowed to naturalize, producing great sweeps of single colour or intricate effects when allowed to mix. Even in small gardens, crocuses can be planted around the base of a tree or encouraged to weave their way through a border. Dainty, rabbit-eared *Narcissus cyclamineus* or the hoop-petticoat daffodil (*N. bulbocodium* var. *conspicuus*) both look lovely naturalized in short grass. The starry *Anemone blanda*, which is available in pure white or shades of lilac blue, can spread in just a few years to form a complete carpet of colour that will last for several weeks. Try combining it with the charming snake's head fritillary (*Fritillaria meleagris*) and the cuckoo flower (*Cardamine pratensis*).

Spring-flowering trees and shrubs
The most spectacular of these are probably the magnolias. If you do not have space for some of the larger species, such as *Magnolia kobus*, with its ivory, water-lily flowers, try one of the beautiful varieties of the star magnolia (*M. stellata*).

Flowering cherries are undoubtedly the epitome of spring and many of these, including the cascading *Prunus pendula* 'Pendula Rosea', are wonderfully graceful trees. To encapsulate most closely the spirit of an authentic cottage garden the best choice may be a fruiting cherry such as 'Morello', which produces snowy white blossom followed by a crop of fruit for cooking.

Many spring combinations look freshest when simply set off by the emerging, new leaves of a deciduous hedge. However, a planting scheme of spring favourites beneath a blossom tree is given an extra dimension when the petals fall confetti-like to mulch the bed below. Try planting dusky purple and slate-coloured hellebores (*Helleborus*) under the candyfloss-pink ornamental cherry, *Prunus* 'Kanzan', or perhaps *Erythronium* 'Pagoda' and trilliums in the shade of the greenish-white *Prunus* 'Ukon'.

Woodland gardens are at their most alluring in the spring before the trees fill the canopy with leaves. Informal woodland plantings of hellebores (*Helleborus*), lungworts (*Pulmonaria*), snowdrops (*Galanthus*) and daffodils, interwoven with candelabra primulas, ferns and other gems such as podophyllums and the Caucasian peony (*Paeonia mlokosewitschii*) are easy to create in shady corners or under shrubs, and require little maintenance.

Containers for spring

Create a spring garden in miniature in a trough or old sink by layering miniature narcissi with species tulips, chionodoxa and crocuses under a carpet of creeping thyme (*Thymus*). The tiny *Narcissus minor* is an enchanting daffodil to plant with hepaticas and gold-laced primulas in a trough. The pasque flowers (*Pulsatilla*) are also excellent for troughs, as their silken buds can be more easily stroked and the jewel-bright flowers are closer to the eye. Combine them with the exquisite, miniature jonquil daffodil, *Narcissus* 'Sundial', or with *N.* 'Segovia', which has white, sugar-paste petals and a flat, lemon-coloured cup. You might like to try some of the dainty species tulips such as *Tulipa* 'Lady Jane' whose white flowers are striped with pink.

ABOVE LEFT: *A spotted form of the Lenten rose (*Helleborus *x* hybrida*).*

ABOVE CENTRE: Narcissus bulbocodium *has dainty 'hoop petticoat' flowers.*

ABOVE RIGHT: Tulipa *'Black Parrot' has unusual, deep wine-black flowers.*

LIFTING AND DIVIDING SNOWDROPS

Snowdrops (*Galanthus*) are often divided 'in the green', meaning when they are in leaf and in flower, usually just as the flowers fade. This technique has the disadvantage of disturbing the roots, but makes it much easier to find the bulbs than if they are dormant under ground, in which case you may accidentally damage them with the spade. Just replant the divided snowdrop clumps in the garden.

1 Find an established clump of snowdrops, dig generously around the roots and lift the clump with a spade or trowel.

2 Gently tease apart the clump either into individual bulbs or small groups, trying not to damage the roots.

3 Replant the bulbs, spacing them at least 5cm (2in) apart in prepared holes 10cm (4in) or more in depth.

4 A handful of garden compost or composted bark helps the bulbs re-establish on heavy soil. Firm the soil and water in well.

the cottage garden in summer

It is difficult to imagine a better way to spend an afternoon than relaxing while listening to the sound of bees among the flowers. The summer garden is not always so soothing, as there are many jobs to be done, but enjoying the sights, scents and sounds of the season is very therapeutic.

ABOVE: Pelargonium 'Polka', one of the Unique Group which flowers from late spring to early autumn.

RIGHT: *This pink summer border shows the uplifting colours and magical effect of dense planting.*

BELOW LEFT: *Blue lupins (Lupinus augustifolius) form an effective contrast of shape and colour to* Rosa 'Iceberg'.

BELOW CENTRE: Verbascum olympicum *has attractive rosettes of woolly leaves and tall spires of flowers.*

BELOW RIGHT: Rosa 'Bantry Bay' is a reliable climbing rose which flowers all summer long.

Cottage-garden favourites

Summer is a season of great profusion, with flowers massed against a background of rich green leaves. Traditional cottage-garden favourites, such as astrantias, hardy geraniums, Jacob's ladder (*Polemonium*) and poppies (*Papaver*), mingle together to give a colourful, informal display. More dramatic accents are provided by spires of flowers like hollyhocks (*Alcea rosea*), delphiniums and verbascums.

For a successful plant combination, the individual elements of colour, shape and texture must work together to create a satisfying whole. These elements may be similar to form a harmonious partnership or they can contrast to produce a more dynamic effect. A summer combination of roses and clematis, for example, can achieve a relaxed garden picture. For example, you might pair *Rosa* 'New Dawn', which has pale pink, fragrant flowers, with silvery-mauve *Clematis* 'Silver Moon'.

Roses are indispensable in summer for their scent and the authentic, cottage-garden look that they bring. Old-fashioned roses, such as *Rosa* × *odorata* 'Pallida', are the ones that most enchant people – the best have a perfume richer than any other. The other essential summer scent comes from the honeysuckle (*Lonicera*), which will attract moths on warm, still evenings. Planting simple flowers like buddlejas, scabious (*Scabiosa*) and stocks (*Matthiola*) in sunny, sheltered borders will encourage summer insects such as butterflies, honey bees, crickets or dragonflies, but use single varieties rather than double ones, which are not open enough for bees to use.

It is not always easy to maintain a continuity of interest after the main display of perennials, such as peonies, columbines (*Aquilegia*) and irises, is over. Think about using lilies (*Lilium*) and

other summer-flowering bulbs, which provide both colour and scent in high summer. The pure white, waxy trumpets of the Madonna lily (*L. candidum*) emit a heady fragrance, while the turk's cap lily (*L. martagon*) adds interest to shady corners. For sheer flamboyance, opt for Oriental hybrids, such as 'Casa Blanca', 'Muscadet' or 'Salmon Star'.

Pelargoniums are another essential summer plant. Red geraniums were popular with cottagers as windowsill plants, but many others would also have been grown. The old *Pelargonium* 'Lord Bute', for example, with its deep wine-coloured flowers, looks exquisite in combination with the silvery heliotrope, *Heliotropium arborescens* 'White Lady'. Growing frost-tender perennials such as these in pots ensures that they can be brought inside easily when the weather starts to cool.

Self-seeders

Some of the best summer partnerships arise by chance when plants are allowed to self-seed. If you stop deadheading in the last part of the summer, then the final flowers of the season have time to dry and the seeds can ripen.

Traditional cottage-garden annuals such as the delicate love-in-a-mist (*Nigella damascena*) or the cornflower (*Centaurea cyanus*) are always appropriate, in combination with diaphanous, pastel larkspurs (*Consolida ajacis*) or mixed with the more vibrant colours of hybrid antirrhinums and begonias. Other self-seeding favourites include California poppies (*Eschscholzia*), pot marigolds (*Calendula officinalis*), candytuft (*Iberis*) and alyssum (*Lobularia maritima*). Columbines and poppies can be used to fill any gaps in the borders.

Foliage effects

The texture and colour of foliage can be effectively combined. Garden pinks and carnations (*Dianthus*) have spiky leaves with a bluish bloom, making an effective backdrop to the flowers. The beautiful bronze fennel (*Foeniculum vulgare* 'Purpureum') has aromatic foliage and is charming when allowed to seed between red and pink roses. Silver-leaved plants such as the curry plant (*Helichrysum italicum*) also work well with pink flowers, creating a soft, feminine effect.

LEFT: *Spires of foxgloves* (Digitalis purpurea) *reach up towards the roses on this rustic pergola – they seed themselves freely, and the seedlings will survive when relocated.*

DRYING FLOWERS FOR USE IN ARRANGEMENTS

There are various methods for drying flowers. Desiccants such as sand, silica gel or even cat litter can be used, and flowers dried in this way retain their shape and colour well. Foliage is often dried in a solution of glycerine, while some flowers can be dried successfully in a microwave oven, although you can't then use flowers that have been wired for floristry. The most usual method is air-drying.

1 Select well-developed flowers and pick them when they are dry, not after rain, otherwise mould may develop.

2 Make small bunches of flowers and tie them together near the base of the stems with an elastic band or string.

3 Hang the flower bunches upside down in a warm but not sunny, airy place, such as an airing cupboard or kitchen.

4 Leave the bunches undisturbed until they are dry. Most flowers will take around two weeks to dry completely.

the cottage garden in autumn

In many ways autumn is the most colourful season of all. There is a wide range of plants to be enjoyed, flowering from late summer through to the first frosts and beyond, but there are also the autumn colours provided by leaves, as well as a great diversity of fruits, hips and seedheads.

ABOVE: *Many of the Japanese acers have beautifully delicate leaves and rich autumn colours.*

RIGHT: *The colours of autumn leaves cast an orange and yellow glow over the garden, but there is still plenty of green interest and flower colour – the* Euonymus alatus *in the right foreground has striking red/pink 'berries' with orange seeds.*

Mellow fruitfulness

The term 'autumn colour' conjures up images of red and gold acers, yellow birches (*Betula*) and russet brown beech trees (*Fagus*). These colours are often repeated in autumn fruits, such as pumpkins and gourds, crab apples, and the berries of hollies (*Ilex*) and barberries (*Berberis*). There is a softer side to autumn, however, with the gentle pinks of many autumn-flowering plants, such as viburnums and the lovely *Prunus* x *subhirtella* 'Autumnalis', which will produce flowers at intervals from early autumn right through until spring.

Autumn favourites

Plant choices that give distinction and impact in the autumn season are extensive. The asters include some of the most dependable of autumn-flowering plants in a range of colours, mostly at the purple end of the spectrum. They form lovely harmonies with violet verbenas and the russet tones of fading hydrangeas. Dusky pink sedums are invaluable for their solid flowerheads, which are so attractive to the last of the season's butterflies.

Contrasting colours can be found in the bright orange seedheads of the Chinese lantern, *Physalis alkekengi* var. *franchetii*, which has creamy white, nodding flowers in summer. Chinese lanterns look appealing among large, orange pumpkins, and are excellent in seasonal flower arrangements. There are also vibrant yellow rudbeckias, while chrysanthemums cover almost the whole colour spectrum. Of particular interest to flower arrangers are unusual chrysanthemum cultivars, such as 'Shamrock Green', with a fascinating form and intriguing colours. It is the Korean and Rubellum types – for example, 'Emperor of China', 'Mary Stoker' and 'Clara Curtis' – that are of most use to the cottage gardener, being good border plants that provide weeks of colour without any cosseting. The chrysanthemums with the warmest colours, such as the Korean 'Agnes Ann', with double, plum-red flowers, and rust-red 'Rumpelstilzchen', associate well with many dahlias, particularly 'Bishop of Llandaff', deservedly popular for its purple foliage and bright red flowers.

Autumn-flowering bulbs

Pinks and white are the dominant colours in bulbs such as cyclamen, colchicums and autumn crocuses. These are more robust than they look, and can be used in sweeps of colour at the edges of plantings of asters and Japanese anemones (*Anemone x hybrida*). In mild climates, or in sheltered places such as a sunny courtyard, you can try many other autumn-flowering bulbs. The autumn snowdrops, *Galanthus reginae-olgae* and *G. peshmenii*, are interesting harbingers of the late-winter snowdrop season. Related to snowdrops are the snowflakes, of which there are autumnal species, including white *Acis autumnalis* and pink *A. rosea*. Autumn daffodils include the Moroccan species, *Narcissus broussonetti*, with its white, scented flowers; *N. serotinus*, with white, star-like flowers; and the fascinating *N. viridiflorus*, with spidery, deep green flowers that smell of cloves. The South African nerines are not scented, but they command attention with their dramatic, floral fireworks.

Seedheads and grasses

The too-tidy gardener may miss out on such seasonal treats as seedheads, which provide interesting textures to contrast with late flowers. The globes of the opium poppy (*Papaver somniferum*) complement the pearly discs of honesty (*Lunaria*). Other seedheads include those of love-in-a-mist (*Nigella damascena*), ornamental alliums (*Allium rosenbachianum*) and the bright orange beads of the stinking iris (*Iris foetidissima*). Grasses can be a particular delight in autumn because they dry into feathery mounds of soft-textured flowerheads that beg to be caressed.

ABOVE LEFT: *The fluffy seedheads of astilbes can last for weeks.*

ABOVE CENTRE: *Rudbeckias provide rich colours in the autumn.*

ABOVE: *The delicate Cyclamen hederifolium will self-seed.*

SAVING TOMATO SEEDS FOR NEXT YEAR'S PLANTING

Saving your own seed is an old cottage tradition, since most cottagers could not afford to buy new seed. Many heritage cultivars of vegetables have survived, but remember that some newer varieties are F1 hybrids, which will not come true from saved seed. Most seeds are fairly easy to dry and save, but tomato seed may be more difficult to extract because it is surrounded by a gel.

1 Scoop out the seeds and gel from the tomato and put them into a glass jar. Leave the jar in a warm place for 4–7 days. It will start to smell yeasty, indicating that fermentation is occurring.

2 A layer of mould will form on the top. Remove the top layer of mould and pulp. Rinse the seeds thoroughly in a sieve (strainer) or by tilting the jar carefully under a running tap.

3 Spread the seed on a plate to dry and leave for about three days until it has dried thoroughly before transferring the seed to named packets in preparation for sowing them later.

4 If you are saving seed from less fleshy fruits, such as these chilli peppers, then you just need to spread out the seeds and dry them in an airy place.

the cottage garden in winter

Snow and frost bring a touch of magic to the garden, especially a hoar frost, which can transform the dullest of dormant shrubs into a crystalline sculpture. Simply leaving the seedheads on plants such as sedums and teasels allows spectacular ice pictures to form when conditions are suitable.

ABOVE: *Cotoneaster fruits can last well into winter before being taken by birds.*

RIGHT: *The framework of bare trees and shrubs is enhanced with a covering of snow.*

FAR RIGHT: *Here a glass cloche is used to protect delicate winter bulbs from the worst of the frosty weather.*

BELOW LEFT: *Fluffy seed heads of clematis earn it the common name of Old Man's Beard.*

BELOW CENTRE: *Crocus* tommasinianus *shrugs off the effects of frost and snow.*

BELOW RIGHT: *Japanese quince will flower from late winter right through to spring.*

Clever choices for winter

Good form and structure, both in the hard landscaping and in the choice of plants, is vital for a beautiful winter garden. Satisfying plant associations should include evergreen plants for structure, colour from bark or flowers and, perhaps most importantly, scent to lift the spirits. Traditional, cottage-garden evergreens include yew (*Taxus*), holly (*Ilex*) and box (*Buxus*), any of which can be used in hedging, as specimen plants or clipped into topiary.

Plant trees or shrubs with attractive bark, such as strawberry trees (*Arbutus*), *Acer griseum, Stewartia sinensis* and the Tibetan cherry (*Prunus serrula*) whose trunk shines like burnished copper. Silver birches are graceful trees with great appeal; *Betula utilis* var. *jacquemontii* has strikingly white bark. Willows (*Salix*) and dogwoods (*Cornus*) can be pollarded to encourage brightly coloured, young stems. The corkscrew stems of the hazel, *Corylus avellana* 'Contorta' are particularly distinctive.

Winter shrubs

Reliable, winter-flowering shrubs include *Elaeagnus pungens* 'Goldrim', which has lustrous, dark green leaves with gold margins and small, silvery flowers that last until mid-winter. Amenable to clipping, it can be shaped into balls and pillars, or trained against a wall. The Christmas box (*Sarcococca confusa*), with glossy, evergreen leaves, makes its presence known in winter with the perfume from the ivory flowers. The much-loved *Daphne mezereum*, with magenta and white flowers with a heavy fragrance, is a cottage classic for doorways. There are also

such as *M. x media* 'Charity', have shiny, evergreen foliage and spires of fragrant, lemon-yellow flowers.

If you want winter-flowering plants to flourish, use the shelter of a wall. The yellow jasmine (*Jasminum nudiflorum*) responds well to the extra protection, and will start to flower as early as late autumn in favoured spots. Clematis are also interesting winter-flowering plants. Varieties of *Clematis cirrhosa* have delicate leaves and nodding, bell-like flowers. *C. c. var. purpurescens* 'Freckles' is a cultivar with creamy tepals, liberally splashed with burgundy.

Winter flowers

Hellebores (*Helleborus*), such as the acid-green-flowered stinking hellebore (*Helleborus foetidus*) and the many colours of *H. x hybridus*, are some of the best loved winter-flowering perennials. Their nodding heads combine well with other late-winter delights such as snowdrops (*Galanthus*) and *Cyclamen coum*, which comes in a range of deep and pale pinks, and white.

Mix in some early Reticulata irises for beautiful blues. *Iris* 'Harmony' has flowers of a mesmerizing pure blue, or the robust hybrid *I.* 'George' has royal purple flowers. Use as many winter aconites (*Eranthis hyemalis*) as you can afford; a great drift of these yellow buttercups is uplifting on a cold winter's day.

the witch hazels (*Hamamelis*), with fascinating, spidery flowers that are often subtly fragrant. *H. x intermedia* 'Pallida' has sulphur-yellow flowers and a sweet scent, while *H. x intermedia* 'Diane' has flowers the colour of a robin's breast and flame-red autumn leaves. The honeysuckle, *Lonicera x purpusii* 'Winter Beauty', is less colourful, but its flowers have a sweet fragrance and continue from early winter to spring. *Mahonia japonica* and its hybrids,

LEFT: *The rosettes of the humble cabbage look attractive in frost — the cabbage, along with Brussels sprouts, broccoli, kohlrabi, leeks and parsnips are hardy vegetables that tolerate a light winter frost.*

PROPAGATING HARDWOOD CUTTINGS

Hardwood cuttings are very easy to take and require little in the way of aftercare. They can be taken at any time during the dormant season, from autumn to spring. This method is ideal for deciduous shrubs, roses, and fruit bushes such as currants and gooseberries, but it can also be used to propagate a number of glossy-leaved evergreens such as holly (*Ilex*) and rhododendron.

1 Select some mature shoots of the current season's growth and cut them with secateurs (hand pruners) — stems that are about the thickness of a pencil are ideal.

2 Cut into lengths of 15–20cm (6–8in) long. Make a sloping cut at the top of the shoot and a straight cut at the bottom, to distinguish which way up the cutting should go.

3 In general, you should cut just above a leaf node (the point at which a leaf emerges) at the top and on a node at the bottom. Gather small bunches of shoots and secure with a rubber band.

4 Insert the cuttings into the ground in a sheltered spot, such as an unused bed or at the back of a border. Keep about a third of the length below the surface. The roots will form along the stem.

familiar features

Cottage gardens can be as idiosyncratic as their owners, but there are certain features that give these gardens a classic and defining style. This chapter identifies the general elements that give the cottage garden its framework. Profuse planting may be the most obvious feature associated with the style, but other characteristics include a feeling of enduring tradition in the hard landscaping, with the use of natural materials, such as stone, cobbles or slate, as appropriate to the locality, and in the use of hedges, walls and trellis to create a sense of enclosure. The cottage garden is not the place for gleaming aluminium furniture; handmade, rustic or old ironwork benches are more at home here. While garden ornaments may well be found (even including the tongue-in-cheek use of a garden gnome or two), a simple stone bird bath or sundial would be appropriate as a strong hallmark feature rather than a formal statue.

LEFT: *An arch overflowing with roses makes an eye-catching and charming feature in a cottage garden.* ABOVE LEFT: *The garden gate sets the tone for the cottage garden: a wooden picket gate is a classic choice.* ABOVE CENTRE: *An ornamental bird bath hidden in the foliage gives local birds a secluded place to bathe.* ABOVE RIGHT: *Traditional water butts and galvanized watering cans are undeniably charming, though you may opt for the cheaper and more practical plastic versions.*
LEFT: *Aegre lascivius saburre adqu ireret syrtes. Gulosus zothecas syrtes* ABOVE CENTRE: *Aegre lascivius saburre adqu ireret syrtes. Gulosus zothecas syrtes* ABOVE RIGHT: *Aegre lascivius saburre adqu ireret syrtes. Gulosus*

boundaries & divisions
Walls, fences and hedges have various roles, including the confinement of livestock and the definition of garden plots as well as a sense of seclusion. Boundary structures also provide support for a range of climbing plants and, of course, encourage the exchange of plants over the garden fence.

ABOVE: Natural planting, including Michaelmas daisies (Aster x frikartii) and iris (Iris pallida), suits this paling fence.

BELOW: Low box hedging is often used to divide different sections of a cottage garden – this staggered design breaks up the formality of straight lines.

BELOW RIGHT: Rustic-looking wattle hurdles are ideal boundaries for use in a rural setting.

Primitive walls

Dry stone walls are usually found in areas with a ready supply of natural stone. They provide nesting sites for birds and roosting holes for bats. In the past they were cheap to make, but, nowadays, a scarcity of skilled craftspeople means that building new walls can prove an expensive undertaking. Old stone walls are often colonized by a range of plants. Sunny walls attract plants such as wallflowers (*Erysimum cheiri*), red valerian (*Centranthus ruber*) and snapdragons (*Antirrhinum majus*), while shady walls may be home to a range of ferns.

Old brick walls are also very appealing, especially when covered with mosses and lichens. However, new brick walls can look stark and so are best softened with climbing plants. Use sturdy vine eyes in the cement to hold taut wires for supporting your climbing plants, or fix wooden trellis to the wall. Attach the trellis to vine eyes, for easier removal, or use blocks of wood to create a gap behind the trellis, so twining stems are not damaged.

Boarded or metal fences

There is a wealth of fencing styles to choose from. Close-board fencing, made from overlapping boards, is often used in the cottage garden, and is probably the best choice if you want privacy. White picket fences, made from vertical wooden pales spaced along horizontal rails, look attractive with plants such as bleeding hearts (*Dicentra spectabilis*) and black-eyed Susan (*Thunbergia alata*) spilling through the gaps. Old, hoop-topped, metal fences have a similarly nostalgic appeal.

Traditional post-and-rail fences are perfect for rural areas and suitable for containing horses and alpacas. For smaller livestock, animal-proof boundaries can be made using chain-link mesh attached to wooden posts. An alternative type of fence can be created using wattle hurdles. These are panels of interwoven woody stems that can be bought ready-made. Although not long-lasting, they provide useful protection while a new hedge is becoming established.

Cottage-style hedges

Living boundaries are the most wildlife-friendly form of barrier, often containing a variety of plants and supporting a range of wildlife. They allow the wind to filter through, therefore providing a better windbreak than a solid boundary, with less turbulence on the leeward side. If you are planting a new hedge, consider what species to use. A productive hedge, for example, calls for species that provide berries or nuts, such as hazel (Corylus avellana). For a dense hedge with year-round privacy, evergreen plants such as holly (Ilex) and yew (Taxus) are ideal. Single-species hedges, perhaps made from beech (Fagus), can look beautiful (and beech, when clipped, retains its brown leaves all winter), but the most wildlife-friendly hedges usually contain a mixture of four or five different native species, including at least one that is evergreen.

Hedges can be planted as single rows or in a staggered double row for a denser hedge. Plant short lengths of hedge by preparing a planting trench along a line of string. For substantial lengths of hedging, the most practical method is slit planting, which involves making a slit in the soil and firming in the plant with the heel of your boot. For pot-grown evergreen plants, pit planting (in which individual planting pits are dug) is the best

option. Once planted, hedges will establish more quickly if they are mulched to conserve water and reduce competition from weeds. In areas where rabbits or deer are a problem, protect the young stems with spiral guards. Wait until late winter to trim established hedges so that birds have a supply of berries and seeds in the autumn. Yew and box (Buxus), however, are exceptions as they benefit from being cut in late summer.

ABOVE: *Fencing and area divisions in the cottage garden are likely to be informal – here we see metal fencing with a built-in arch and a low picket fence.*

FAR LEFT: *Woven panels with open features allow plants to peep through.*

LEFT: *Clematis are among the most popular climbers – this one blends beautifully with the weathered texture of a stone wall.*

the garden gate

As a functional feature, the garden gate keeps pets, livestock or children inside and the rest of the world out, and yet it signifies more than this. It hails the beginning of the cottage garden experience and the perimeter of your domain, and allows passers-by to catch beguiling glimpses of the garden beyond.

ABOVE: *Open metalwork gates such as these give tantalizing views of the garden beyond.*

RIGHT: *Lychgates are often seen in churchyards and also have considerable charm at the entrance of a cottage garden.*

BELOW: *This traditional wooden picket gate casts dramatic shadows over the stone garden pathway.*

Pastoral gates

The most common cottage-garden gate is the traditional paling or picket gate made from vertical boards nailed to a strong, diagonally braced frame. The wood used may be larch or chestnut, except for the hanging post, which should be made from a hardwood such as oak. Make sure that any gate is properly braced with the diagonal strut running from the top by the latch down to the bottom by the hinge. In the days before pressure-treated timber, the wood might have been coated with tar or linseed oil, or painted white, grey or green.

Simple metal gates can look just as attractive as wood and will last longer. While a rusty patina gives a more rustic effect, metal gates should be painted regularly to keep them in good condition – black, white, cream or pale green or blue can all look effective.

In rural locations, kissing gates are useful in a larger garden, especially between the garden and any land that is used for grazing livestock, as these gates are stock-proof.

They can have a basic V-shaped or rectangular design, or be semi-circular if they are made from metal. A traditional, wide-field gate is recommended if you need access to the garden with large vehicles. These classic farm gates usually have five or six horizontal bars. Gates leading from the garden to the fields are usually rustic in appearance, but the main garden gate may be a decorative feature in its own right, with the paling tops cut into ornamental shapes.

Wrought-iron work

While metal gates are widely available, many at reasonable prices, much cheap ornamental ironwork is made from a mild steel. Genuine wrought iron is much more durable and products made of this should be guaranteed to last over 300 years. One option would be to commission a wrought-iron gate from a local blacksmith. This could be expensive, but will give you an individual product and will also support a local craftsperson. Salvage yards can also be a good source.

Encircling planting

The gate is the point at which you first catch a glimpse of the garden, and so it is common to use the space around the gate to hint at what lies beyond. Arches can be used over the gate to facilitate a casual planting of scrambling roses (*Rosa*) and honeysuckle (*Lonicera*). Alternatively, plant climbers such as clematis, jasmine (*Jasminum*) or, in warm areas, *Dregea sinensis*, which has downy, heart-shaped leaves and nodding heads of fragrant, creamy flowers that are speckled with pink.

If the gate is set in a hedge, the hedging plants on each side can be trained to form a living archway over the entrance. Yew (*Taxus*), box (*Buxus*), escallonia or pyracantha all work well, but you can also use scented plants such as elaeagnus or osmanthus to great effect. Scented shrubs like daphne could also be included on either side of the gate. Even a simple planting of annual flowers, such as mignonette (*Reseda odorata*), wallflowers (*Erysimum cheiri*) or night-scented stocks (*Matthiola longipetala* subsp. *bicornis*), provides a welcoming fragrance.

Plants with cheerfully coloured flowers at the gate will lift your spirits, as well as those of passers-by. Try sowing nasturtiums (*Tropaeolum majus*) so that they will scramble through the hedge and around the gate. The traditional mixture of orange, yellows and reds is always effective, or you could try a more unusual variety, such as 'Strawberries and Cream', which has creamy coloured petals, splashed with strawberry pink.

Smooth maintenance

Check the hinges of your gates from time to time to ensure that they are running smoothly and are showing no signs of rust. Wooden gates will require an annual treatment of diluted linseed oil (this seals the wood while also allowing it to breathe), or the occasional new coat of paint. Gates hung from posts rather than attached to a wall or brick piers may eventually need replacing as the posts may rot if the wood has not been suitably treated.

BELOW LEFT: *A sturdy ironwork gate contrasts with, and accentuates, the soft colours and textures in the planting.*

BELOW: *A wooden arched gateway creates a delightfully romantic view of the garden beyond, framed with roses and honeysuckle.*

the garden path
Whether a straight line running from the gate to the cottage door, a meandering trail between beds brimming over with flowers or providing access to the vegetable patch, the path sets the style pace. Thus, the materials and design of a path need to be charming, practical and harmonious with the cottage-garden ethic.

ABOVE: *Simple brick paths are a practical way of dividing up beds in the vegetable garden.*

OPPOSITE TOP LEFT: *The slight curve of this stone pathway increases the sense of informality.*

OPPOSITE MIDDLE LEFT: *Bark chips are suitable for covering paths that are less frequently used.*

OPPOSITE BOTTOM LEFT: *Brick paving and decorative square tiles provide an attractive feature and a safe foot passage for plant maintenance.*

RIGHT: *Here slate chippings are used as an infill between stone slabs – the purple tones of the chippings combine beautifully with the Geranium 'Nunwood Purple' at the path border.*

FAR RIGHT: *Bricks laid in a herringbone pattern draw your eye down the line of the path.*

Designing a cottage-garden path
Choosing the route the path is to take can be an enjoyable process. You can mark a route with a trail of builder's sand, or use a garden hose or canes and string. In snowy weather you can walk a trial route and then look back to see how your footprints have traced the course.

Make sure that the path will be wide enough, particularly if you plan to use wheelbarrows. If you want plants generously spilling out of the borders and over the path, allow extra space for this. A path of 90–120cm (3–4ft) across is probably a comfortable minimum width.

In the past, paths might have been made from beaten earth, hearth cinders, broken pots, stones or even the shells of nuts. Such paths can get muddy and slippery, and are little used today.

Gravel is a popular material: it has a warm appearance, making it an effective backdrop for plants. Adding a low edging, such as timber gravel boards, bricks or terracotta edging tiles, will prevent the gravel migrating into the borders. The depth of gravel used is important: too little, and the gravel quickly disappears into the soil; too much, and the surface can become difficult to walk on. Lay the gravel over a weed-suppressing membrane to prevent it working into the soil.

Cobbled paths are common in areas with a plentiful supply of flint and are attractive when they have developed a mossy growth, although also slippery. Combine the cobbles with bricks or slabs to create decorative patterns. They are perhaps more wisely used for secondary paths around the garden rather than the main thoroughfare, which demands a more even surface.

Brick paths can be expensive to lay. They are, however, a good investment because they are hard-wearing and long-lasting. Ensure that the bricks are frost-proof or they may start to crumble after a couple of hard winters. The bricks can

be laid in straight lines or in a variety of patterns, such as basketweave or herringbone. Lay the bricks against a gravel board so that they do not move out of line as they settle.

Concrete paths can be unappealing in their dull grey state, although you can add powdered iron to the cement to produce a terracotta-type colour. They are relatively cheap and easy to lay, as well as hard-wearing and easy to maintain. A concrete path is a practical choice in frequently used areas such as the vegetable garden or potting shed. If the concrete is made with a fairly large aggregate and then brushed with a broom before it sets, a more aesthetically pleasing result can be obtained, as well as a more slip-proof surface.

Path definition

Edging the path draws the eye along it and provides a note of restraint in contrast with the tumbling chaos of the borders. Pathways were often lined with just one variety of plant, such as double daisies (*Bellis perennis*), pinks (*Dianthus*), white alyssum or blue lobelias. While the popular image of a cottage-garden path is one with plants flopping over the edge, you may wish to use short, woven willow hurdles to restrain the plants. Other suitable edgings include bricks set on their ends, terracotta edging tiles, and, more informally, large flints, cobbles or cockleshells. If the path is regularly used for wheelbarrows or wheelchairs, ensure any edging is sturdy enough to withstand being knocked.

ABOVE: *Herbs such as lavender planted alongside the path will release their fragrance when passers-by brush against them.*

LAYING A BRICK PATH

Brick paths can be laid on a bed of sand over a hardcore base or, for a more robust path, a bed of mortar. Laying on mortar also reduces weed growth in the cracks. A well-prepared base of hardcore, levelled with ballast, is important if the path is likely to be subjected to heavy wear. This path uses a basketweave design; other options include running bond and herringbone.

YOU WILL NEED:
- Pegs
- String
- Spade
- Rake
- Gravel boards
- Wooden pegs
- Hardcore
- Wooden board for compacting
- Lump hammer
- Bricks (the number will depend on the size of the path)
- Piece of wood
- Builder's sand
- Garden broom

1 Mark out the route of the path with pegs and string. If you can, adjust the width to fit the brick size because you can then avoid cutting the bricks to fit. Position gravel boards on each side of the path and hold these in place with wooden pegs.

2 Using a spade, dig down along the length of the path by approximately 15–20cm (6–8in), working out the precise depth according to the depth of the chosen bricks. Level the ground with the back of a rake.

3 Put a layer of hardcore over the raked soil base and firm in well. Add a layer of sand, approximately 8cm (3in) deep. Rake the sand evenly and compact thoroughly with a lump hammer.

running bond brick design

herringbone brick design

basketweave brick design

4 Lay the bricks on the sand following your chosen brick design, ensuring that there are no gaps between them. Use a lump hammer on a piece of wood to level them.

5 Brush dry sand into the joints between the bricks.

6 In shady situations such as this algae may build up on the bricks making them slippery. Treat with an algaecide, available from pond suppliers.

cottage climbers

Abundant, freeflowing roses clambering around the door and wisteria draped across the walls create a spectacular cottage-garden statement. Whatever plants you use and whether for a door or other arch, aim for a sensuous combination of layered forms with resonant colours and delightful scents.

Making an entrance

The front door is the most obvious focal point when you are viewing the garden from the gate. Traditional cottage doors were made from simple planks, using hardwoods such as oak that were treated with linseed oil or allowed to silver with age. Other types of wood should be painted, using a fairly restrained colour so that the surrounding planting commands the attention. As well as climbers, the cottagers of old would also have planted small, scented shrubs such as daphnes and wintersweet (*Chimonanthus praecox*) by the door so that their fragrance could be enjoyed as they went in and out.

Climbing plants may be trained against the house wall by the door, and over the entrance porch, if you have one. Simple porches are easy to construct using an arch made from woven willow or trellis. To erect a trellis archway, fix trellis panels at right angles to the wall against vertical battens. A depth of 60cm (2ft) or so gives enough space to shelter visitors at the door. Most climbing plants require a rich soil to sustain vigorous top growth, so, if necessary, replace the soil near the door with a good topsoil enriched with well-rotted manure or garden compost. The passion flower (*Passiflora*) is a useful exception: it thrives on poor, stony soil, if it gets plenty of sun.

Choosing the right climbers

When making decisions about which climbers to plant, research their potential growth. Climbing plants that look innocuous in a pot at the garden centre can become rampant thugs once established in the ground. Similarly, if you would like to plant the ubiquitous rose around the door, select a climbing rose rather than a rambler, because these can be too vigorous, quickly covering a large area. Climbing roses often have quite stiff stems, but they are usually fairly easy to train and generally have large flowers; many will also repeat-flower over a long season, unlike ramblers.

TOP: Rosa *'Madame Alfred Carrière' is a climbing Noisette rose which is happy in sunshine or shade.*

ABOVE LEFT:
A flamboyant display of climbing roses and spires of delphiniums creates vibrant colours.

ABOVE RIGHT: *The large flowers of climber Clematis 'Perle d'Azur' can last for many weeks in summer.*

ABOVE: *Rambling roses have a profusion of flowers but can be difficult to train.*

ABOVE RIGHT: *Almost all clematis are climbers, but they can have many different flowering habits – the large flowers of Clematis 'Mrs N Thompson' appear late in the season.*

RIGHT: *Wisterias are hardy, long-lasting and vigorous climbers – especially distinctive for their heavy clusters of pendulous flowers.*

SUITABLE CLIMBING PLANTS

Different cultivars of species vary greatly in their vigour so if in doubt clothe small structures with delicate climbers such as the late-summer flowering *Codonopsis vinciflora* or *C. grey-wilsonii*, rather than a rampant plant that may smother its support.

TWINING PLANTS
- *Akebia*
- Black-eyed Susan (*Thunbergia*)
- *Clematis*
- Honeysuckle (*Lonicera*)
- Jasmine (*Jasminum*)
- Morning glory (*Ipomoea*)
- *Wisteria*

Akebia

SCRAMBLING CLIMBERS
- *Bougainvillea*
- Brambles and hybrid berries (*Rubus*)
- *Plumbago*
- Rambling roses

Plumbago

TENDRILLED CLIMBERS
- Chilean glory flower (*Eccremocarpus scaber*)
- *Cobaea scandens*
- Grape vines (*Vitis vinifera*)
- Passion flower (*Passiflora*)
- Sweet peas (*Lathyrus odoratus*)

E. scaber

Good choices are the velvety crimson *Rosa* 'Etoile de Hollande' or the thornless 'Zéphirine Drouhin', which has deep rose-pink, very fragrant flowers. 'Pink Perpétue' is a more modern introduction that has clear pink flowers over a long period. 'Mme. Grégoire Staechelin' flowers only once, but gives a magnificent display of rich pink, scented blooms. The bronze-yellow, richly fragrant flowers of 'Maigold' can look particularly good against a brick wall. 'Penny Lane' is a more compact climber, so you are less likely to need ladders when training it.

Clematis climbing through rose stems creates a classic cottage-garden partnership. Many of the large-flowered clematis hybrids, such as 'Peveril Pearl' or 'Alice Fisk', flower at the same time as the main flush of roses, or you can choose one of the later-flowering *Clematis viticella* hybrids, such as 'Gipsy Queen', to carry on the display as the roses finish. Climbing honeysuckle (*Lonicera*) is available in many species and the flowers are highly perfumed. Woodbine (*L. periclymenum*) has reddish, fragrant flowers and is less likely to take over than *L. japonicum*.

For fragrance, *Mandevilla laxa* has shiny, rich green leaves and pure white, scented trumpets from mid-summer into autumn. It is not reliably hardy and needs a sunny aspect. Mulch around the base in cool areas to provide winter protection. *Trachelospermum jasminoides* is a strong, twining climber with fragrant, whirling, ivory flowers. It looks lovely in combination with the purple potato vine, *Solanum crispum* 'Glasnevin'.

ERECTING A TRELLIS FOR CLIMBERS

Plants such as ivy have aerial roots by which they can attach themselves to any vertical surface. Other climbing plants, such as clematis, passion flowers and morning glories, require support. Mounting trellis panels on a wall provides a climbing structure for such plants.

YOU WILL NEED:
- Trellis panels (with dimensions to suit the size and shape of the door)
- Wood stain or paint
- Wooden battens (approximately 50 x 25mm/2 x 1in)
- Rawl plugs
- Screws (approximately 50mm/2in long)
- Well-rotted manure or garden compost
- Fork
- Spade
- Suitable climbing plants, such as *Dregea sinensis*, *Schisandra rubiflora* or sweet peas (*Lathyrus odoratus*)
- Vine eyes and wires
- Watering can

1 If the trellis is untreated, paint it with a suitable exterior wood stain or paint.

2 (top right) Fix wooden battens or blocks to the wall to enable the trellis to stand slightly proud of the wall, leaving an air gap. This allows the plants to grow through and makes subsequent

maintenance easier. For brick walls, drill holes into the mortar, at least 35mm (1½in) deep, and insert a rawl plug (or a similar device) before attaching the battens with screws. Battens spaced about 90cm (3ft) apart along the length of the trellis will provide enough support for heavy climbers.

3 Screw the trellis panels to the wooden battens or blocks.

4 Plant the chosen climbers at the base of the trellis in well-prepared ground. Wind the stems of twining plants through the trellis, tying them as necessary to secure.

5 Continue to wind the stems through the trellis. Here vine eyes and wires are used to extend the plants beyond the top of the trellis. Water the roots in well.

seating

A cottage garden looks unfurnished without at least a couple of seats, preferably one positioned in a sunny spot and another in the shade, so that you can choose where to sit. Admittedly, the busy gardener may not spend much time sitting on a bench, but visitors can use it as a vantage point from which to enjoy the garden.

TOP: *This rustic bench is constructed from logs.*

ABOVE: *A stone-topped bench complements the surrounding vegetation.*

ABOVE RIGHT: *A pink-painted wooden bench mirrors the rose's colour.*

Rustic benches and seats

A traditional cottage-garden seat might have been made from two stout logs with a simple plank placed across them. In a modern cottage garden we usually want something a little more comfortable to maximize leisurely contemplation. The same applies to dining furniture; in the past, cottage-garden furniture would have been homemade, but unless you're a skilled carpenter, it's best to buy ready-made tables and chairs. Wood and wrought iron are attractive, traditional materials for use in the garden, and all-weather cane furniture can also look good. Even some types of plastic can blend in, if you choose them carefully.

Large, sophisticated garden benches can look out of place in a cottage garden where a more simple, rustic design would be suitable. Deck-lounger-type seats are ideal for lazy summer days, but a sturdy bench is perfect if you simply want somewhere to sit and admire the garden or chat to friends. For romantic trysts, a mossy bench or loveseat in a shady arbour is called for, while a small table and chairs in a sheltered corner also make for a useful sanctuary.

Recycled and homemade options

Scouring secondhand shops or auction rooms may produce garden furniture that is far more fitting than a new, garden-centre purchase. Look out for old, French-bistro-style furniture, which is usually quite compact, readily portable and easy to use

in a small garden. Redundant church pews can make ideal garden benches, while even old school desks can be pressed into service as unusual seating.

In tiny courtyards, benches can be built against the walls so that they take up less space than free-standing ones. A bench could be constructed in an alcove by securing timber rails to the wall and putting planks of wood across to form the seat. Use brass or galvanized screws to prevent them from rusting.

If you are building raised beds in the garden, you could make the retaining walls wide enough to be used as seating.

The English poet John Clare (1793–1864) urged cottagers to build garden seats amid sweet briars and other scented flowers. If you wish to surround a garden seat with fragrant roses, remember to plant them well back from the seat or choose a thornless cultivar such as 'Madame Legras de Saint Germain', 'Zéphirine Drouhin', 'James Galway', 'Tea Clipper' or, in honour of the poet, 'John Clare'.

Hammocks for lounging

The ultimate in garden relaxation is stretching out in a hammock. While not a classic feature of the hard-working cottage garden, it creates a casual atmosphere that works with the often chaotic style of flowers and vegetable beds. If you do not have suitably spaced trees, you can purchase support stands, but they are a poor relation to an arboreal hammock. If there is only one tree of a suitable size, then use a robust post as the second support. Add an attractive finial to the top and train sweet peas (*Lathyrus odoratus*) or other scented climbers around it. Simple, classic hammocks are shaped like a sling, but they are also available with rod spacers at each end, which can make them more comfortable. The ideal spacing between supports should be approximately 60cm (2ft) more than the whole length of the hammock when measured from ring to ring.

ABOVE LEFT: *A love seat in an S-shape has two sections and is perfect surrounded by soft planting in a relaxed corner of the garden.*

ABOVE CENTRE: *This low wooden bench is simply made from railway sleepers.*

ABOVE RIGHT: *Spend a lazy summer day relaxing in a hammock and enjoying the sights and sounds of the garden around you.*

FAR LEFT ABOVE: *These Adirondack chairs are a comfortable option for garden furniture and fit well in a rural setting.*

FAR LEFT BELOW: *An ornate cast-iron bench creates a nostalgic style of faded grandeur in the front courtyard of this romantic garden.*

arches & arbours
When made as a simple rural structure, arches give a contrasting vertical note among low plantings and provide the opportunity to grow climbing plants. While arbours are often associated with grander gardens, they also work in a cottage garden, when planted with fruiting vines and scented flowers.

ABOVE: *This arch is covered with* Rosa wichurana *'American Pillar', a fast-growing, large-flowered climber.*

BELOW LEFT: *Wisterias entwine themselves around a loggia and a climbing rose creates an exuberant arch.*

BELOW RIGHT: *Arches create secret areas and entrancing views – this metal archway is covered with blue* Cedrus atlantica *'Glauca' (Atlas cedar).*

OPPOSITE: *Alternate dense planting with light planting to give variation to a pergola pathway and vista.*

Arches for height and romance

The cottage-garden arch may originally have been designed to echo the style of the lychgate at the local church. The lychgate is a porch-like structure over the gateway with a roof that is often covered in thatch or wooden tiles. The roof often has spiky wooden finials to prevent the devil from sitting on top. In today's cottage garden, simple arch designs look most effective, particularly when the structure is bare in the winter.

Arches can be used to provide a focal point or to invite visitors to pass through to a different part of the garden. They are also useful for adding height to a small or flat garden, as well as for marking the division between two sections of a garden or where two paths cross. They can be used to frame a view out of the garden to the landscape beyond or to draw attention to a particular feature within it. If you have sufficient space, you might also like to erect a series of arches over a path to provide a shady tunnel, very similar to a pergola. Indeed, a vine-covered pergola is often seen in cottage gardens, providing a shady spot for a bench and the opportunity to grow grape vines (*Vitis vinifera*).

Arbours for shade and shelter

Originally simply a seat surrounded by a trellis structure over which plants were grown, arbours can bring a sense of seclusion to the garden and enable you to sit in comfort, shielded from the wind. Arbours covered in grapevines were once a common feature in many colonial gardens in the United States and are popular now in many old-fashioned gardens. Nowadays, virtually every garden centre seems to stock a selection of different, off-the-peg arbour designs, some of which are quite open with just a trellis surround, while others are totally boarded, giving greater protection from inclement weather (although these have less of a sense of sitting among the flowers). In some arbours, the seat doubles as a box store for keeping garden tools, whereas others have a swing seat for greater relaxation.

Construction options

Arches and arbours can be made from either metal, such as wrought iron or aluminium, or from wood. Rustic poles, made from larch or fir, are also used. The bark can be left on for a rough finish or stripped off for a smarter effect. Vertical supports need to be about 10cm (4in) in diameter and can be either set in concrete or sunk into the ground to a depth of around 50cm (20in) for stability. The ends should be soaked in a wood preservative before the structure is assembled. The main cross beams should be made from poles at least 8cm (3in) in diameter. Thinner poles can then be used to fill in a latticework.

The easiest way to build an arch is to buy a kit, which comes with the posts and beams cut to size. Once installed, you can stain the wood in colours such as pale green, blue or dove grey.

ABOVE: *A wooden arbour enveloped by climbers and other greenery creates a romantic feature, and a dreamy seat where you can feel close to the rhythms of the garden.*

ABOVE RIGHT: *In a larger garden, a simple green arch forms an inviting natural boundary from one area to another.*

Cedar and chestnut woods are resistant to decay, but softwood structures will need regular treatment with preservatives – a challenge if there is a mass of planting over the structure. Metal arbours are more costly, but are often made from weather-resistant, powder-coated steel and will last for years without any maintenance. Willow arbours are easily and cheaply made using cut stems of many willow (*Salix*) species. They mature quickly, but the woven stems look attractive from the start.

Green arches

Create an arch from living plants by training trees or tall shrubs together, planted on either side of a path. A more formal structure can be created by pleaching trees. This involves training the side branches to meet in parallel, horizontal lines and then interweaving the new growth to form a vertical screen. Beech (*Fagus*), lime (*Tilia*) and hornbeam (*Carpinus*) were traditionally used for this, but hawthorn (*Crataegus*) also works well and looks lovely in the spring when scattered with blossom. You can also create living arbours by hollowing out mature plants, such as yew (*Taxus*), box (*Buxus*) or privet (*Ligustrum ovalifolium*), using appropriate topiary techniques.

Arching climbers

When selecting climbing plants for an arch or arbour, consider the location of the structure. Many flowering shrubs and vines need at least six hours of sun each day, but some roses, such as 'Teasing Georgia', 'Golden Showers' and

'Veilchenblau', can cope with shadier positions. Good roses for arches include 'Goldfinch', with gold to primrose-yellow, scented flowers, the almost thornless, apricot-yellow 'Ghislaine de Feligonde', and the brilliant red 'Allen Chandler', a repeat-flowering climber that was much loved by the garden writer Beverley Nichols (1898–1983).

Roses for pergolas need to have a fairly lax growth: 'Phyllis Bide' with dainty, yellowish flowers; apricot-yellow 'Crépuscule'; and white 'Snow Goose' are well worth considering. Other flowering vines to use include wisteria, jasmine (*Jasminum*), honeysuckles (*Lonicera*), clematis, and, in mild climates, the trumpet vines (*Campsis*). For autumn colour, plant the Virginia creeper (*Parthenocissus quinquefolia*) or the spectacular, crimson glory vine (*Vitis coignetiae*), which has leaves the size of dinner plates.

Do add in a fruiting vine or two. Grapevines (*Vitis vinifera*) are classic plants, which would have been planted by cottagers so that they could make their own wine, but sweet dessert grapes such as the seedless cultivars 'Reliance' and 'King's Ruby' are also popular. Kiwi fruits (*Actinidia deliciosa*) are a good alternative because they have scented, ivory flowers followed by delicious fruits, as long as you have male and female plants or choose a self-fertile cultivar such as 'Jenny'. Even the canes of blackberries and hybrid berries can be trained up an arch, allowing easy picking of the fruit. Choose a thornless cultivar such as *Rubus fruticosus* 'Oregon Thornless' or the Buckingham tayberry, which does well even in a frosty site.

MAKING A WILLOW ARBOUR

Willow arbours are simple garden structures to make during the winter and usually establish quickly, as long as you keep the willow well watered in its first season. If you want to create a scented bower, plant honeysuckles such as *Lonicera* x *americana*, with golden-yellow, rose-flushed flowers, or *L*. x *heckrottii* 'Gold Flame' before putting in your willow stems or rods.

YOU WILL NEED:

- Shrubs and climbers to grow through the arbour
- Approximately 24 willow stems or rods, around 3m (10ft) long, for uprights
- Approximately 12 willow stems for horizontal strengtheners
- String or waxed twine to tie the willow stems together

1 Consider the size of seat you wish to have in your arbour. Lift the turf to form the U-shape of the arbour and plant out any shrubs or climbers that will be used to weave through the arbour.

2 Cut a supply of long willow stems, approximately 3m (10ft) in length, from a coppiced or pollarded willow. Alternatively, you can order them from a specialist supplier.

3 Push two stems into the ground at either side of the front edge so that 15cm (6in) is in the soil. Tie them together at the top to form an arch. Push in the rest of the stems to create a semi-circle. Tie together at the top.

4 Weave stems horizontally in and out of the vertical stems to strengthen the structure.

5 You can either weave the stems in a fairly random way or use a basketweave technique for an attractive, more formal effect.

6 Water in well. Apply pressure to the horizontal stems to help them bend without breaking and then twist the ends back on themselves to neaten the front edge of the arbour.

7 Keep the willow well watered throughout the first growing season to encourage them to root and grow away vigorously. Protect the stems from deer or rabbits if necessary.

8 As new shoots form, weave them in to create a dense structure which should mature over a period of 2–3 years.

topiary

From spirals to stylized hens and peacocks, the art of topiary has flourished in cottage gardens for hundreds of years. Probably first practised in imitation of specimens seen at the manor house, topiary continued to be popular with cottagers even when the fashion all but disappeared from grander gardens in the early 18th century.

ABOVE: *The shape of the fountain is echoed in the topiary behind.*

RIGHT: *Low box hedging is expanded to form intriguing sculptural shapes – soft swathes of planting offset the more tailored shapes.*

BELOW: *This carefully trimmed yew (Taxus baccata) is a unusual distinguishing feature of the cottage frontage.*

BELOW RIGHT: *Here, box (Buxus) is carefully clipped to form decorative enclosed areas for other plants.*

Topiary shapes and designs

As far back as Roman times, plants were clipped into sculptural shapes such as obelisks or, more fancifully, into animals. In the Far East, the Japanese art of cloud pruning has a similar, if more solemn, appeal. Traditional cottage gardens often featured a single topiary specimen, treated as a 'living heirloom', with the plant and the techniques for maintaining it being passed down the generations. Today, topiary shapes in the cottage garden are fairly simple, predominantly globes, cones, spirals, cottage loaves and a variety of animals. Large-growing plants such as yew (*Taxus*) can be made into larger topiary features such as tunnels or summerhouses.

The best plants for topiary are evergreens, such as box (*Buxus*), yew (*Taxus*), holly (*Ilex*), phillyrea and myrtles (*Myrtus*), because these retain their form all year round. Privet (*Ligustrum ovalifolium*) and *Lonicera nitida* are also used. The latter two grow quickly, so they will require frequent trimming to keep them in shape. Privet also loses most of its leaves in cold winters.

Caring for topiary

The frequency of clipping depends on the species, the growth rate in any given season and the design. Yew is normally clipped once a year, box generally requires two clips, and fast-growing species like *Lonicera nitida* may require three clips. Very intricate box designs may need trimming every four to six weeks. Clipping is usually undertaken between early summer and early autumn, although it may be necessary throughout the year in warm climates.

Apart from clipping, the routine care of topiary is similar to other shrubs. Keep them weeded and water thoroughly during prolonged dry spells in the first year. Apply a balanced fertilizer or liquid seaweed-based feed two or three times during the growing season. In winter, knock off any snow from plant surfaces so that it does not damage the main framework.

Basic topiary clipping

Shaped wire cages are sometimes used to make clipping shapes easier, but the cottage gardener often relies on a steady hand, a good eye and plenty of patience to achieve the

same effect for less cost and greater satisfaction. Rounded topiary shapes are much easier to form than more angular pieces. Clip the shape with whatever tool feels most comfortable, whether this is scissors, secateurs, hand shears or sheep shears. Electric hedge trimmers can be used for large, simple shapes.

ABOVE LEFT AND RIGHT: Topiary animals were used in the cottage garden in imitation of grander gardens, and bring a touch of humour.

HOW TO TRAIN A TOPIARY STANDARD

Buy a mature, dense, bushy plant with a defined upright stem at the centre. This plant must be the correct height for the final standard as it will fill out rather than grow taller. The treatment may seem rather drastic, but the head soon starts to develop ready for further shaping.

1 Cut off all the branches emerging from the base of the plant to leave one single upright stem with side shoots along its length. Remove most of the side shoots up to the base of the proposed head, but retain a few feathery leaf shoots to help the main trunk to grow in strength.

2 Begin to shape the head by shortening the side shoots to form a rough ball. Cut out the shoot tip of the leading growth to encourage side shoots to form. Then pinch out other shoot tip buds with your thumb and forefinger.

3 Tie the stem to a vertical cane that reaches to the base of the ball of shoots. Continue shaping the head to the desired shape as it grows. Give the plant some slow-release fertilizer to encourage growth, and water well. Stand in a sheltered spot away from direct sunlight and wind.

4 When you are clipping the final shape, flip the shears over so that the blades follow the curve of the ball. Keep an eye on the shape and continue to pinch out any leaves or shoots that appear on the stem or the leg of the standard to keep the circular shape clearly defined.

small ponds & water features

In a cottage garden water had to serve a purpose, whether as a well to supply water or as a pond to provide a water store in case of fire. Simple birdbaths were often included and, if there happened to be a natural stream, it would have been used as a home for ducks or geese.

TOP: *A shallow dish with water and pebbles makes an informal bird bath.*

ABOVE: *A well, once an indispensable utility, is still an attractive ornamental feature.*

ABOVE CENTRE: *Even the smallest pond will attract frogs and dragonflies to your cottage garden.*

ABOVE RIGHT: *This quirky, mosaic-lined bird bath is sure to draw in avian visitors.*

Cottage garden ponds

Including water in the garden adds another dimension to the plot, increases the range of plants that can be grown, and encourages a variety of wildlife to visit, including water boatmen, dragonflies, frogs, toads and kingfishers. Natural sunken ponds will often have an irregular shape with a gently sloping bank to allow easy access for livestock. Ponds in cottage gardens are likely to be bordered with natural materials such as turf, cobbles or stones. If you do not already have a pond, you can build one using either a pre-formed fibreglass pool or a heavy-duty plastic liner such as butyl.

The inclusion of marginals, which thrive in shallow water, and moisture-loving plants around the edge of the pond will soften its outline. Marginals prefer different depths of water, but, in general, they require 8–15cm (3–6in) of water above their crowns. Suitable plants include the flowering rush (*Butomus umbellatus*), with rounded heads of pink flowers, the yellow flag iris (*Iris pseudacorus*) and the marsh marigold (*Caltha palustris*). Plant marginals and open-water plants such

water lilies (*Nymphaea*) in aquatic planting baskets, which have open lattice sides to allow water and gases to circulate through the planting mix. If the holes in the planting basket are very large, it is best lined with a material such as hessian (burlap), so that the soil does not wash out.

Elongated ponds or streams may benefit from the installation of a bridge. Simple plank bridges look most appropriate, but they can be slippery in wet weather, so cover them with wire netting to provide better grip. Install a handrail if the bridge is to be used regularly by children or the elderly. These can be made by threading lengths of rope through holes drilled in vertical posts or larch poles. Make sure that any wood used for the bridge is treated to prevent the wood from rotting.

Oxygenating plants are important for the ecology of the pond as they release oxygen into the water during daylight hours. Many oxygenating plants such as Canadian pondweed (*Elodea canadensis*) can become invasive, so do take advice from a reputable pond supplier.

Pond maintenance

Many aquatic plants spread rapidly, forming dense mats of vegetation that inhibit the flow of a stream or quickly fill a pond, so cleaning out and removing plant growth regularly is essential. Take out blanket weed (*Spirogyra*) by inserting a bamboo cane into the weed and twisting it round the stick. Leave water plants or weed by the side of the pond for a day or two before composting to allow aquatic animals to return to the pond.

Informal water features for small gardens

In a small garden it is still possible to have a water feature, even if it is simply a stone birdbath covered with lichens. You can also use containers such as half-barrels or large, glazed pots or urns, as long as any drainage holes are sealed with a silicone sealant. Some metal containers can be toxic to fish and plants, however, so seal them first with a rubber paint. With small volumes of water, the temperature changes may be too great to keep fish, but such containers are suitable for a few special plants such as miniature water lilies (*Nymphaea*). *N. tetragona* 'Helvola' is the best water lily for tubs, producing a succession of lemon-yellow flowers. For contrast, you could include the miniature bulrush (*Typha minima*) or the corkscrew rush (*Juncus effusus* 'Spiralis'). In warm climates or with winter protection, you could even try one of the smaller lotus cultivars, such as *Nelumbo nucifera* 'Momo Botan', which has double, peach-coloured flowers.

BELOW LEFT: *A natural-looking pond for an informal garden.*

BELOW: *Even a water butt is likely to be visited by birds and dragonflies.*

BOTTOM: *A small stone bird bath nestles among lady's mantle (Alchemilla).*

decorative features

With a country emphasis and dense plantings of old-fashioned flowers, cottagers would not have used garden statues and ornamental items – the utilitarian would have taken precedence. However, the modern-day cottage garden has moments of fancy, using primitive or distressed materials and rural symbols.

ABOVE: *Old plant labels tucked behind a crossbar create a casual decoration, while also reminding you exactly what you have planted.*

RIGHT: *Brighten up workaday areas with a collection of everyday objects that have taken on a patina over time.*

BELOW RIGHT: *Battered agricultural equipment looks charming when casually placed among the flowers.*

OPPOSITE: *Delicate vertical features with scrolled metal flourishes give height and a growth structure for the roses, and contribute to an enchanting garden scene.*

Charming focal points

Striking statues and pieces of decorative sculpture serve the practical purpose of creating a focal point in the garden, a resting point for the eye amid the exuberance of the planting. Statues and sculpture benefit from a light dressing of vegetation, at least until they have been in the garden long enough to have developed a rich growth of lichens. Try draping female statues with a necklace of the jewel-like flowers of *Tropaeolum tricolor, Rhodochiton atrosanguineus* or one of the climbing species of codonopsis such as *C. grey-wilsonii*. Willow or trellis obelisks can also be used to add height and interest to the garden. They can be as much a focal point in the winter when dusted with snow as in the summer when used as a support for climbing plants.

If you buy just one decorative feature, then a sundial combines a long history with practicality and beauty. The most common is the horizontal sundial, easy to read and usable all year round. These are usually mounted on a natural stone pillar and positioned at the end of a pathway or as an accent in a border. They are seen in formal herb gardens, perhaps surrounded by a planting of thyme (*Thymus*) as a visual pun, and often inscribed with a motto.

Horizontal sundials consist of a flat-dial plate inscribed with hour lines radiating from the centre and an upright gnomen, which casts a shadow on to the dial face when the

sun shines. The gnomen is usually fixed relative to the dial face and, in the northern hemisphere, must point towards true north. In order for you to use a sundial to tell the time accurately, it must be designed for the latitude of your area, although a sundial designed, for example, for a latitude of 40° can be used at a latitude of 45° if the plate is tilted upwards by 5°. However, many mass-produced sundials are not designed to be anything other than ornamental.

Cottage-style *objets d'art*

Many practical objects, such as terracotta rhubarb and sea kale forcers, Victorian glass cloches and bell cloches, also have appealing sculptural qualities. In the same way, you often see galvanized metal watering cans, buckets and coalscuttles used as props to enhance the ambience of a cottage garden. Terracotta wall plaques featuring traditional images, such as the green-man motif, may be seen on garden walls or outbuildings, and collections of horseshoes are also popular.

ABOVE: *Storage jars and tins from another era can be salvaged to make delightful vases and plant pots.*

ABOVE CENTRE: *Rusty iron machinery blends surprisingly well with the russet hues of many ornamental grasses.*

ABOVE RIGHT: *Metal buckets that have seen better days can be given new life as containers for plants.*

Salvage objects

The *objet trouvé* (or found object) popularized by Marcel Duchamp in the early 20th century was really nothing new. Cottage gardeners had always recycled redundant objects, because they did not have the money to buy new. Today, as more people are becoming aware of the environmental impact of throwing away old possessions and buying new ones, salvage and reuse is as important as ever.

Finding salvage items will often be serendipitous, like a chance conversation revealing a source of unwanted church pews. Otherwise search reclamation yards, visit garage sales and car boot fairs and spend time beachcombing.

Agricultural items such as animal feeding troughs can be used for water plants or collections of alpine and rock garden plants if they have drainage. Old sinks may be used for the same purpose. The stone ones are hard to find, but white, glazed Belfast sinks are as functional and a stone finish can be simulated easily using a hypertufa mixture. This is an artificial medium that sets to a rock-like consistency. It can be made by mixing one part sharp sand to one part Portland cement and two parts peat or a peat substitute. Water is added to give a porridge-like mixture, which is then used to cover the glazed sink or even polystyrene (Styrofoam) boxes.

Other items to use as plant containers include old leather gardening boots for sempervivums and old wellington (rubber) boots for strawberry plants or tumbling tomatoes. Search the kitchen cupboards for cracked or chipped china for planting flowers, or cookie tins that can have drainage holes punched into the base. Unwanted colanders or sieves can be made into hanging baskets. Other domestic items such as galvanized metal baths can be turned into water features, while laundry buckets and enamel washing-up bowls may house a small waterlily.

Display tables

Old mangles (wringers) or sewing machine tables can make attractive display tables on which to arrange plants in pots or a collection of seashells, stones or fir cones. They look effective against a house or outbuilding wall because of their domestic associations. Cast iron or wirework étagères for displaying plants are occasionally seen, but can be expensive. A cheaper option is to use an old wooden stepladder or set of kitchen steps; as long as the treads are reasonably wide they can support a number of pots of plants.

Auricula theatres

Many grand gardens in the past had an auricula theatre, a series of tiered shelves set into an alcove on which to display special pot plants such as show auriculas (*Primula auricula*). The auricula theatre at Calke Abbey in Derbyshire, England, is one of the few original ones still surviving. The aristocracy were not the only ones who wanted to show off their precious plants, and many cottage-garden florists also built staging for their favourite flowers. Some were elaborate and even had curtains to protect the plants from bad weather.

CREATING A PLANT DISPLAY SHELF

A display unit for small plants, which is similar to the auricula theatres of grand houses in the past, but much simpler, can be made from an unwanted picture or mirror frame. It can then exhibit a collection of small treasured plants such as auriculas, anemonella cultivars, snowdrops or reticulata irises grown in individual pots. If you do not have a suitable frame, scour secondhand shops and car boot sales for something appropriate, or make one out of wooden planks or old wine boxes.

YOU WILL NEED:

- Old mirror or picture frame
- Wooden planks or boards, approximately 10cm (4in) wide
- Weather-proof wood glue
- Metal brackets
- Fine tacks
- Wood primer
- Selection of auricula plants
- Weather-resistant wood varnish
- Sturdy brackets

3 Assemble the box using a weather-proof wood glue and metal brackets. Attach to the frame with glue and fine tacks.

4 (left) Cut out a central shelf and attach it to the box with brackets.

1 Carefully take off the back panel from the frame and remove the mirror or picture.

2 Using planks or boards, approximately 10cm (4in) wide, cut two long and two short sides to create a box that will fit the aperture of the frame.

5 If the original frame has a suitable back panel, then you can use this to form the back of the box. Alternatively, you will need to use lengths of planking cut and glued together. The back panel can now be attached to the box.

6 Prime the wood and paint the inside of the box. A matt-black paint makes a good backdrop for the jewel-like colours of auriculas. Coat the frame and the outside with a weather-resistant varnish. Fix to an outside wall, using sturdy fixings.

trees, flowers & shrubs

A traditional cottage garden contains plants that envelop you in colour and fragrance – to help you make choices for your garden, this chapter shows you some of the options. To create maximum impact and a reliable display, include core plantings of reliable cottage-garden stalwarts, such as foxgloves (*Digitalis*), campanulas and penstemons. Boost this with flashes of spontaneous brilliance from cheerful, self-seeding annuals. Create layers of interest using trees, shrubs and other plants, weaving together the ornamental ones with productive plants such as fruit trees and vines. Size is important; there are cottage-style plants appropriate for the smallest garden, window box or patio pot, providing the scents, colours, textures, flavours and sounds required for an uplifting, sensuous cottage garden that will leave a lasting impression.

LEFT: *Shrub roses combine to good effect with biennial foxgloves (Digitalis purpurea) and annual Love-in-a-mist (Nigella damascena).* ABOVE LEFT: *Trees bring a sense of timelessness to the garden and a fruit tree has different guises, from spring blossom through to the maturing of its fruit harvest.* ABOVE CENTRE: *This packed border has a colourful mix of perennial plants.* ABOVE RIGHT: *Starflowers (Anemone blanda) are tolerant of a variety of soil types and naturalize easily.*

beds & borders
Long borders filled with summer-flowering perennials are a feature of many country gardens, but cottage-garden beds and borders tend to be created in a more relaxed way, with an eclectic planting mix that gives a longer season of interest. Borders will also often contain a selection of fruits, vegetables and herbs.

ABOVE: *Perennials and annuals combine with bulbs such as ornamental onions in this harmonious cottage-garden border.*

BELOW: *Flagship spires of lupins (Lupinus) lead the eye into a crowded display of foliage and flowers, including favourites such as roses and hardy geraniums.*

One-sided borders
A garden border is often backed by a wall, fence or hedge, which provides a firm line to work against and contributes to its overall appearance. If the backdrop is a wall or fence, trellis or vine eyes and vines can be attached to it, and climbers can be grown up them. Establishing a border alongside a hedge is more difficult, because the hedging plants will compete with the new plantings for water and nutrients. Hungry shrubs are best planted at a distance of 60–90cm (2–3ft) from the hedge, but many annuals and perennials will happily grow close to it.

Classic borders often have a clearly defined structure. The plants are carefully graded so that tall specimens, such as delphiniums and hollyhocks (*Alcea rosea*), are at the back, progressing to short edging plants like pinks (*Dianthus*) at the front. A more informal look can be achieved by allowing some taller plants to grow at the front of the border. Semi-transparent screens of taller plants such as grasses or the Russian sage, *Perovskia atriplicifolia* 'Blue Spire', soften the front line, while allowing the colours of plants further back to shine through.

Garden designers often insist on plants being grouped in batches of three, five or seven to create a natural planting effect. It is up to the individual gardener to discover what works best, but including large groups of each plant produces a more restful scene than dotting plants individually through a bed or border. However, the use of random planting and allowing favourite plants to self-seed throughout the borders produces a wonderful, mille-fleur effect.

SOWING SEEDS IN PREPARATION FOR GERMINATION AND PLANTING

Sowing seed and watching the new seedlings emerge can be an exciting process. Use a special potting mix designed for seed as the high levels of nutrients in some mixes can inhibit germination. For the seeds of trees, shrubs and alpines, which can take a while to germinate, mix in a proportion of loam-based potting mix. This will give the pot or seed tray more stability and make it easier to re-wet the potting mix if it dries out. Cover with a layer of horticultural grit in order to reduce the growth of mosses and lichens.

   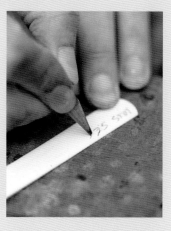

1 Fill the pot or seed tray with potting (soil) mix. Level off and firm down, either with a block of wood, the base of another pot, or the back of your hand. Water well and allow to drain.

2 Sprinkle the seed evenly over the surface of the potting mix. Spreading the seed out ensures that the plants will not be in competition with each other too quickly.

3 Cover with a thin layer of potting mix or horticultural grit to the depth recommended on the packet. Very small seeds such as begonias may be better left uncovered.

4 Add a label with the seed name and sowing date. Put hardy plants in a cold frame or sheltered corner until germination. Keep tender plants on a warm windowsill or airing cupboard.

Island beds

An island bed is one that is seen from all sides, usually in the middle of a lawn. Beds may be any shape or size, flat or raised above ground level. Raised beds are usually contained with timber or brick walls. They are often used for low summer bedding, but can have more impact if they include a permanent feature such as a small tree, a shrub or a climber-clad obelisk. Long beds and borders, in particular, benefit from the use of obelisks, pieces of topiary or other sculptural plants, which form punctuation marks within the beds. Successful plants or groupings can be repeated at intervals down the border to provide a sense of rhythm.

Don't be afraid of a chaotic bed with an informal design, often the trademark of the cottage garden. Aim for plantings that will be dense at maturity – and if spaced close together, the lack of bare soil won't allow room for weeds. Plants can also be encouraged to self-seed through the bed and any seasonal gaps could be filled with young plants of annuals or fast-growing perennials such as penstemons. Alternatively, plants such as dahlias and lilies can be grown in pots and then plunged into any gaps as they are coming into flower.

LEFT: *Ornamental cabbages freely placed within a border create a dazzling colour combination within this bedding display.*

If the ground is reasonably moist, shrubs such as rhododendrons and Japanese maples (*Acer palmatum*) will thrive, while perennials such as primroses (*Primula vulgaris*), rodgersias, wood anemones (*Anemone nemorosa*), trilliums, lily-of-the-valley (*Convallaria majalis*) and ferns can be used as ground cover. In Britain, the quintessential plant for woodland is the English bluebell (*Hyacinthoides non-scripta*), whose bulbs yield starch that was used in Elizabethan times to stiffen ruffs. Avoid the Spanish species, *H. hispanica*, as it hybridizes with the English species and in some areas threatens wild colonies.

In drier shade there is a more limited range of plants that can be grown successfully, but foxgloves (*Digitalis*), ornamental nettles such as *Lamium maculatum*, the sweet violet (*Viola odorata*) and *Iris foetidissima* are reliable stalwarts. A dependable plant for the dry, root-bound shade under trees is the charming *Cyclamen hederifolium*, also known as sowbread. Plants self-seed to form a beautiful carpet of marbled leaves with dainty pink or white flowers in autumn.

Some interesting forms of the wild strawberry will flourish in shade and in limy soils, making good ground cover. The Plymouth strawberry, *Fragaria vesca* 'Muricata', is an oddity that was found by John Tradescant in a garden in Plymouth, England. It has greenish flowers and intriguing, small, narrow fruits that are covered with green hairs. 'Variegata' has attractive cream-and-green variegated leaves that remain through all but the severest winters, but it produces little fruit. There is a double-flowered form, 'Flore Pleno', and an eccentric form, 'Monophylla', which has just a single leaf rather than the usual tripartite strawberry leaf.

ABOVE: *Creamy roses and ivory* Hydrangea arborescens *'Annabelle' combine with a fulsome hedge outside Anne Hathaway's Cottage in Stratford-upon-Avon, England.*

RIGHT: *Use a more freeflowing planting design to create informal beds with the feel of a wild flower meadow – here ornamental grasses and ice plants (*Sedum spectabile*) suit a sunny location with dry, sandy soil.*

Rose beds

Few plants can rival roses for their range of colours and fragrances. In formal gardens, they are often grown on their own, but a rose bed can look bleak when you are not in the main flowering season. A more cottagey effect can be obtained by underplanting the roses with plants like Siberian irises (*Iris sibirica*) or some of the less vigorous hardy geraniums. The soft blue of catmint, *Nepeta* 'Six Hills Giant', makes an excellent natural companion to roses, as do astrantias such as 'Ruby Wedding'. Early-flowering roses such as the yellow *Rosa xanthina* 'Canary Bird' look lovely underplanted with bulbs of violet-blue *Scilla peruviana*. Many herbs such as rosemary (*Rosmarinus*) and lavender (*Lavandula*) may be planted with roses, or you can try growing them with vegetables such as Swiss chard.

To add height and structure to a rose bed, train climbing roses, such as *R*. 'The Garland', on posts or obelisks. With a rectangular rose bed, you could even have a post at each corner joined by swags of rope festooned with roses, making the ultimate four-poster rose bed.

Shade-lovers

Many traditional cottage-garden plants appreciate a sunny site, but if you want to create a cottagey border in shade you can seek inspiration from woodland situations. The shady conditions found beneath tree canopies are home to a variety of plants that can be used to create peaceful, naturalistic effects. Woodland-type borders look best when edged with informal paths made of natural materials such as bark chippings, log stepping stones, pine needles, gravel or hoggin.

FAR LEFT: *A haze of blue in the shade of trees and shrubs gives an uplifting springtime feel to this bed.*

LEFT: *White roses in flower bring a refreshing luminescent cheer to darker areas of the garden.*

PLANTING A DECORATIVE BED

Good preparation is important when planting a new bed. Time spent digging over the ground, removing perennial weeds and incorporating organic matter will be amply repaid later by the extra growth in your new plants and less subsequent weeding. Once you have dug over the planting area, firm the soil well with the heels of your boots and rake it level.

1 Mark out the boundaries of the bed and dig over the ground, removing any weeds. Rake the soil level. Edge the bed as required. Position plants in their pots to check that you are happy with the overall effect.

2 Begin planting the main plants – here, the white Judas tree (*Cercis siliquastrum* f. *albida*). Backfill the soil around the tree and firm in with your heel. Insert a stake at an oblique angle and tie the tree to the stake.

3 Plant any smaller shrubs and herbaceous perennials. Sow the seed of annual plants in the spaces between the permanent plantings. Then, water the entire bed thoroughly.

4 If you have not already edged the bed with brick, then short willow hurdles can be used as an edging at this stage. They look attractive and may prevent any free-range chickens from scratching up new plantings.

classic cottage plants
Ask any group of gardeners to suggest their favourites and you will get a huge range of responses. While some plants will feature more prominently than others, it is perhaps the sheer variety of plants used that most typifies the cottage garden and these personal choices make each one special.

TOP: *The lacy flowers of common elder give promise of elderberries.*

ABOVE LEFT: *This wooden fence supports the clambering fragrant honeysuckle* (Lonicera caprifolium) *and is fronted by a cheerful mix of poppies and columbines* (Aquilegia).

ABOVE RIGHT: *While* Wisteria floribunda *is the only climber here, the* Ceanothus 'Concha' *has spread to create the effect of a climber, with* Hebe hukeana *and* Myrtus 'Glanleam Gold' *growing at the base.*

Trees for practicality and versatility

More than any other plant, trees are truly multifunctional. They may have beautiful blossom, foliage and ornamental bark and can, of course, bear fruit or nuts. Trees also provide shade, structure, a support for climbers, a home for wildlife, and a place to hang a swing or hammock or even to build a tree house.

Trees can be grown in a small garden, but careful selection is needed to ensure that they do not make growing other plants difficult by competing for moisture, nutrients and light. Narrow, column-shaped trees give much needed height without taking up too much horizontal space. *Populus tremula* 'Erecta', the Swedish upright aspen, for example, is commonly used as a street tree in the northern United States, and is also useful in the garden. Some small trees can be grown in containers, which restricts their growth, but they need frequent watering.

Shrubs for structure and enchantment

These important plants give structure to borders and extend the garden's season of interest. There are shrubs in flower in every month of the year, while many dual-purpose plants such as the Japanese quince (*Chaenomeles japonica*) have beautiful flowers followed by interesting fruit. Indispensable shrubs include those with scented flowers like lilacs (*Syringa*), philadelphus and daphnes. The elder (*Sambucus nigra*) has foamy flowers that can be used to make fritters and elderflower 'champagne'. The common myrtle (*Myrtus communis*) is a Mediterranean shrub, sprigs of which were traditionally included in a bride's bouquet. Myrtles flower better after a long, hot summer and will then produce aromatic, purple-black berries that can be used to season pork and game dishes.

Roses for classic romance

Shrub roses are, of course, a ubiquitous feature of the cottage garden, being cherished for their historical associations and often their antiquity, but most of all for their beauty and perfume. It is impossible to resist the velvety petals of 'Tuscany', the purplish-red pompoms of the Portland rose, 'Rose de Rescht', the vigour of the highly scented Bourbon rose, 'Gipsy Boy', or the blackish-red blooms of 'Louis XIV', a China rose. There are also climbing roses for every garden space, from the modest 'Jeanne Lajoie' with miniature, pink flowers to ramblers like 'Paul's Himalayan Musk' and 'Kiftsgate' that send down luxuriant cascades of blooms.

FAR LEFT: Rosa *'Constance Spry'* has cupped soft pink blooms with a good myrrh scent.

CENTRE LEFT: Syringa meyeri *'Palibin'* is not as fragrant as many of the large lilac varieties but is neat enough to fit in any garden.

ABOVE LEFT: Clematis viticella *'Flore Plena'* has charming double flowers in an unusual dusky purple colour.

Climbers: weaving the cottage-garden fantasy

Essential garden plants, climbers grow over arches, through hedges or over the cottage itself. Roses, honeysuckle (*Lonicera*), jasmine (*Jasminum*) and clematis; a cottage garden is inconceivable without them. Wisterias are probably the most revered of all climbers. They look stunning if allowed to climb through a mature weeping willow (*Salix*), but can also be grown as standards or paired with pink *Clematis montana* to scramble over a bank.

Climbing plants are not only ornamental. Grapevines (*Vitis vinifera*), for example, are decorative plants that bring shade to pergolas, but also produce a useful crop. There are many cultivars that can be grown outside of the Mediterranean-type climatic regions with which they are most associated. Try the virtually seedless, green dessert cultivar 'Perlette', or perhaps 'Dornfelder', which produces huge bunches of dark red grapes. 'Boskoop Glory' is a reliably hardy grape cultivar; it produces almost seedless black grapes.

TAKING SOFTWOOD CUTTINGS

Softwood cuttings are taken in spring or early summer when new shoots from the parent plant are beginning to harden. Semi-ripe cuttings taken in late summer are less prone to wilting, but may be slower to root. Here *Ceratostigma willmottianum* is used.

1 Take cutting material from the current season's growth. Most stems root quickest at the nodes (leaf joints), so trim just below a node. The length of the cuttings can vary, but is usually between 5–12cm (2–5in). Strip away the lower leaves to give a clean stem for inserting in the potting mix.

2 Dip the cuttings in rooting hormone, which contains auxins to stimulate root growth and often fungicides to prevent infection of the cuttings. Many species, however, will root perfectly happily without this.

3 Insert the cuttings in a pot of well-drained potting (soil) mix and cover with a plastic bag, inverted wine glass or plastic bottle to maintain humidity. Rooting times vary greatly, but a good root-ball should form after six to eight weeks; you will know when you see new leaves appearing.

4 Separate the rooted cuttings. Pot up each cutting, firming the soil around it well and keeping the potting mix moist, but not soggy, until the plants have established, when they can be hardened off and planted out.

ABOVE: *Cabbages and kale add interesting leaf shape and colour to a border with eryngiums, lilies and the castor oil plant,* Ricinus communis.

ABOVE RIGHT: *Flat lacy umbelliferous plants make an effective contrast to spires of foxgloves (*Digitalis purpurea*).*

Perennials for abundance and colour

It is usually perennials that produce the billowing charm and chaos of cottage-garden beds and borders. Many are valued for their foliage as much as for their flowers. Perennial herbs such as mint (*Mentha*) and fennel (*Foeniculum*) are widely grown in borders and pots. Classic, easy-to-grow plants such as hollyhocks (*Alcea rosea*), columbines (*Aquilegia*) and scabious (*Scabiosa*) are also attractive to bees and butterflies.

Many cottage-garden favourites are simply colour variants of wild plants. The rose-pink form of the wild betony, *Stachys officinalis* 'Rosea', for example, makes an excellent border plant with pretty spikes of flowers. The wild primrose (*Primula vulgaris*) has also given rise to a huge number of cultivars, many of which have been treasured for hundreds of years, like the old, double, lilac Quaker's Bonnet (*P. vulgaris* 'Lilacina Plena').

When choosing perennials, consider the conditions that you have to offer them. In a well-drained soil in full sun, peonies (*Paeonia*), Oriental poppies (*Papaver orientale*), furry lamb's ears (*Stachys byzantium*) or pretty springtime pasque flowers (*Pulsatilla vulgaris*) will all flourish. Conversely, primulas, pulmonarias and the bleeding heart (*Dicentra spectabilis*) are best for planting in a damp, shady hollow.

Annuals and biennials for dramatic effect

Indispensible for their ability to bring an impression of established planting in a short space of time, annuals and biennials will give a colourful display in just a season or two

from sowing. Examples include short filler plants such as *Alyssum* and candytufts, through to the statuesque spires of verbascums, foxgloves and teasels. The tobacco plant, *Nicotiana sylvestris,* has scented flowers on 1.5m (5ft) stems. *Cosmos bipinnatus* has large, showy blooms above feathery foliage, whereas *Cineraria* 'Silver Dust' is grown for its silver leaves.

Many of this group can be sown directly in their final positions, but they will be safer from slugs and other pests if sown in modules or small pots and planted out in early summer.

Bulbs to hail the onset of spring

There is something truly magical about spring bulbs. Planted in autumn and forgotten in winter, they suddenly astonish you one spring day with their brilliance. There are bulbs for every season, however, with lilies (*Lilium*), gladioli and dahlias bringing drama to the summer; colchicums, cyclamen and crocuses enlivening the autumn; and winter aconites (*Eranthis hyemalis*), snowdrops (*Galanthus*) and more crocuses enriching the winter.

Bulbs can be endlessly versatile, lending themselves to planting in tubs or window boxes, being woven through beds and borders, or naturalized en masse in grass – to achieve a natural-looking planting, throw handfuls of bulbs on to the grass and plant them where they land. Effective displays can often be obtained from inexpensive bulbs. Generous potfuls of vividly coloured tulips (*Tulipa*), great sweeps of the blue heads of grape hyacinths (*Muscari*) and scattered stars of *Anemone blanda* cost very little to establish.

FAR LEFT: *The Welsh poppy* Meconopsis cambrica *will seed itself around cheerfully in sun or shady places.*

CENTRE LEFT: Geranium *x* magnificum *is one of the taller hardy geraniums with lovely royal purple flowers in early summer.*

LEFT: *Combine the pale* Narcissus *'Hawera' in a bed with polemoniums for a classic and delightful spring display.*

There are bulbs for virtually any situation. Crocuses and cyclamen generally prefer well-drained soils, whereas summer snowflakes (*Leucojum aestivum*) proliferate in damp ground. The fragrant poet's narcissus (*Narcissus poeticus*), colchicums, camassias and snakeshead fritillaries (*Fritillaria meleagris*) all flourish in meadow situations. Snowdrops and English bluebells (*Hyacinthoides non-scripta*) are happy in woodland settings, but the Madonna lily (*Lilium candidum*) and foxtail lilies (*Eremurus*) are best grown in full sun. Bulbs such as gladioli, tigridias and ixias may not survive cold winters but can be planted out in early spring and lifted as the foliage starts to die back in autumn for storage in a frost-free place over winter.

DIVIDING PERENNIALS FOR REPLANTING

Plants are generally divided when dormant in late autumn or early spring, although fleshy-rooted perennials such as agapanthus are often left until their buds are beginning to shoot in spring. Fibrous-rooted plants such as day lilies (*Hemerocallis*) are usually divided using two forks positioned back-to-back. For plants with a woody crown, simply chop through the crown with a spade. Those with loose, fleshy roots such as lily-of-the-valley (*Convallaria majalis*) can be pulled apart by hand.

1 Lift the clump of plant to be divided. Shake off excess soil and insert either one or two forks into the clump. Divide the clump by prising it apart.

2 Improve the soil by digging it over with a fork. As you dig, work in plenty of organic matter. Keep the divisions cool and moist in a shady place.

3 Retain healthy, vigorous sections, planting them at the same depth and trying not to damage the roots. Firm in well.

4 Water the new plantings well and the divisions should re-establish themselves quickly.

container gardening
Growing plants in containers, whether pots, hanging baskets or window boxes, has always been a cottage-garden tradition. This is not only as a means of moving around prized florists' flowers, but also as a way of brightening up windowsills and growing useful herbs close to the kitchen door.

ABOVE: *Potted violas surrounded by a bountiful mass of euphorbia creates an attractive spring feature.*

RIGHT: *Stonecrop (Sedum spathulifolium) grows well in containers and looks attractive even in mid-winter.*

FAR RIGHT: *Marguerite daisies (Argyranthemum frutescens) prefer a position in full sun and flourish in containers.*

BELOW RIGHT: *An ancient stone trough is reinvented as a raised container for a summer begonia display.*

OPPOSITE: *Plants in a cottage garden will typically cover every available area – here, a spectacular display of trailing lobelia (Lobelia erinus) and petunias is created in hanging baskets each side of the front entrance.*

Choices of container
All manner of containers can be used for growing plants, from old buckets to wooden half-barrels, from tall chimney pots to milk churns (though metal containers can get too hot in the sun). Remember that the container should have drainage holes unless you are growing bog or water plants. As a rule, bigger is better: a plant can quickly exhaust the nutrients in the potting (soil) mix in a small pot and will require more frequent watering. It is advisable to use a loam-based potting mix, which has greater reserves of nutrients and is heavier, thus providing more stability. Add a liquid feed to the water once or twice a week during the growing season.

Growing plants in containers also allows you more flexibility in your choice of plants. If you live in an area with limy soil, for example, but are keen to grow acid-loving plants such as camellias, azaleas or blueberries (*Vaccinium corymbosum*), simply plant them in a container of ericaceous potting mix. Equally, you can grow plants such as alpines that require a fast-draining growing medium, even if you have a sticky clay soil, by planting them in troughs or pots of gritty potting mix. You might also wish to experiment with fruit and vegetables, as well as ornamentals. Indeed, plants such as aubergines (eggplants), peppers and tomatoes are perfect candidates for pots on the patio.

Hanging baskets
Cottage gardeners use hanging baskets because they allow a range of plants to be grown even in restricted spaces such as balconies and courtyards. They are also superb for softening the hard lines of buildings, walls and fences and for bringing colour and exuberance to dull corners.

There are many types of hanging basket, from the traditional, open, wirework hemispheres, which require liners to retain the potting (soil) mix, to rustic-looking cones and pyramids woven from plant stems or banana leaves. Open-type baskets are usually lined with moss, which looks attractive and retains moisture well, but there are serious environmental concerns about the large-scale harvesting of moss. A more environmentally friendly option is to use moss raked from the lawn or even preformed cardboard liners, wool waste or old jumpers.

Choose large baskets wherever practical, as they will not dry out so quickly. If the basket does not have an integral polyethylene liner, put a plastic plant saucer at the bottom to help retain water. Fill the basket two-thirds full with a potting mix to which you have added a slow-release fertilizer. Plant upright plants in the middle and surround them with trailing plants, angling them over the edge or through the sides of wire baskets. Fill any remaining gaps with more potting mix and water in well to settle. Subsequent maintenance involves regular watering and supplementary feeding, as well as deadheading the flowers to prolong the display, tasks that apply to all types of container.

ABOVE: *A multi-coloured hanging basket creates a spherical blur of rainbow colours and the promise of a magical garden beyond.*

ABOVE RIGHT: *Strategically placed containers of different heights can create dynamic lines of colour in a patio or courtyard.*

Plant selections

Your choice of plants – a mixture or a single variety – need only be limited by the size of the basket and whether it is in sun or shade. Some unusual possibilities are *Sutera cordata* 'Snowtopia', the poached egg plant (*Limnanthes douglasii*) or a dwarf sweet pea (*Lathyrus odoratus*) such as 'Little Sweetheart' or 'Sugar 'n' Spice'. In shady situations, you could try busy Lizzies (*Impatiens*), streptocarpus and trails of *Rhodochiton*.

Herb baskets are popular for hanging outside the kitchen door for easy harvesting. Many vegetables can also be grown in baskets. Try bushy or trailing tomatoes, such as 'Tumbling Tom Red' and 'Balconi Yellow', or grow a range of cut-and-come-again salad leaves like mizuna and tatsoi. Dwarf French (green) beans work well in baskets and tolerate drier conditions than other crops.

Even fruits such as strawberries and cranberries (*Vaccinium*) can be grown in a hanging basket. Cranberry plants need an ericaceous potting mix and should be watered with rainwater. Strawberries thrive in a loam-based potting

(soil) mix combined with some water-retentive, hanging-basket potting mix. Good cultivars to choose for well-flavoured berries include the French varieties, 'Mara des Bois' and 'Gariguette', and the English-bred, long-cropping 'Everest'.

Window boxes to dress your space

These are invaluable for transforming bare walls and allowing fragrance to waft in through open windows. Window boxes are also fun, allowing you to create a miniature garden. They are available in a variety of sizes and colours, as well as a range of materials, including wood, zinc, copper, steel, wicker and rigid plastics, many of which can be used with a plastic inner liner. There are different brackets to support window boxes, ranging from single potholders to those that feature anti-slip safety devices. Make sure that you have measured your windowsill before buying a window box; also check that the box has holes in the base for drainage.

As window boxes are usually in prominent positions, they need to look attractive over a long season. Try planting a selection of permanent plants for interest all through the year and then add a succession of annual flowers that can be easily replaced when they look past their best. For example, you could plant a pair of box (*Buxus*) globes or cones to give year-round structure and fill in with some spring-flowering bulbs such as the little daffodil *Narcissus* 'Tête-à-tête'. Remove the daffodils when they fade and, for summer interest, plant some trailing, white-flowered *Sutera cordata* 'Snowflake'. In autumn, replace these with cyclamen or winter-flowering pansies such as 'Skyline Yellow Blotch' or the Nature Series.

Edible plants can also be grown in window boxes, facilitating easy picking. Try combining herbs such as basil (*Ocimum basilicum*) with trailing cultivars of cherry tomatoes like 'Trailing Tom Red' and its yellow alter ego 'Baby Rosanna', a short aubergine (eggplant) cultivar with felty leaves, purple flowers and a profusion of tiny fruits. The dwarf runner bean 'Hestia' has bicoloured flowers and stringless beans. There are also compact pepper plants, such as 'Apache' and 'Demon Red', both bearing prolific crops of chillies. Compact sweet (bell) pepper cultivars include 'Orange Baby'.

Scented plants in a window box allow beguiling fragrances to drift into the house. Stocks are ideal for this purpose, including both the double-flowered bedding stocks, such as *Matthiola incana* 'Sugar and Spice', and the night-scented

M. longipetala subsp. *bicornis*. Wallflowers (*Erysimum cheiri*), sweet Williams (*Dianthus barbatus*), heliotrope, marvel of Peru (*Mirabilis jalapa*) and old cottage pinks such as *Dianthus* 'Mrs Sinkins' will all produce wonderful perfumes. For plants to trail over the sides, try morning glories (*Ipomoea*) or moonflowers (*I. alba*), if you have a warm wall. Related plants such as the red morning glory (*I. coccinea*) or the Spanish flag (*I. lobata*) will be equally successful. Black-eyed Susan (*Thunbergia alata*), in shades of orange, apricot and yellow, will look very cheerful tumbling down a brick wall.

Window boxes will house small collections of special plants such as named cultivars of snowdrops (*Galanthus*) in winter or auriculas in springtime. In the summer a collection of cacti or succulents require less watering than other plants and are ideal for awkward-to-access positions.

BELOW LEFT: *This hanging bucket holds a simple but colourful combination of salad leaves and red salvias.*

BELOW: *The pale pastel blooms in this densely planted window box complement the sash window and white shutters, and create a vision of a hazy summer day.*

fruit & vegetables

Whether they are grown in utilitarian rows, muddled in among the flowerbeds or included in an ornamental potager, the growing of fruit and vegetables is a fundamental part of cottage gardening. Although the early cottagers grew their own vegetables, fruit and herbs from sheer necessity, the modern-day gardener also has the opportunity to relish the freshness, flavour and diversity of small-scale garden produce, as well as to take advantage of its economic benefits and convenience. Vegetables, particularly tomatoes and other salad crops, are more widely grown by gardeners than fruits – surprisingly, perhaps, as so many fruits are easy to grow and give a satisfactory crop for years with little maintenance after the initial planting. Try to grow a range of produce in the borders or in pots and hanging baskets, and you will soon appreciate how attractive and flavourful home-grown fruit and vegetables can be.

LEFT: *This vegetable patch makes use of every part of the bed, with tightly packed rows of cabbages, kale, onions and beans.* ABOVE LEFT: *Medlars (*Mespilus germanica*) produce large crops of fruits for making jams and jellies.* ABOVE CENTRE: *The bright stems of chard are planted alongside lettuces and marigolds.* ABOVE RIGHT: *Strawberries are an easy and rewarding fruit to grow in pots.*

the vegetable garden

With its neat rows of crops and hardworking ethic, a vegetable plot is often found at the bottom of the garden. An authentic cottage garden, however, needs to be have vegetables and other edibles at its heart. The joy for today's gardener is that the colour and texture of vegetables creates a dramatic centrepiece.

ABOVE: *A glasshouse is useful for raising young vegetable plants before planting them outdoors.*

RIGHT: *This productive corner of the garden has a fig tree against the wall and vegetables including runner beans, onions and cabbages in the bed.*

BELOW RIGHT: *Using a technique called 'combination planting' vegetables such as courgettes (zucchini) and kale are combined with French marigolds (Tagetes patula) – the latter will repel some insect pests.*

Getting started

Vegetables are usually more productive in a fertile, loamy soil in an open, but not exposed, site. Growing vegetables in narrow beds with a width of not more than 1.2m (4ft), rather than large, open plots, allows for routine care to take place without you walking on the soil. You can also grow vegetables successfully in tubs, troughs or even hanging baskets if space is an issue. When thinking about what vegetables to use, be aware that new cultivars come out each year, but many cottage gardeners prefer to grow old-fashioned heritage cultivars as they may have a better flavour or a more unusual colour or shape than modern cultivars. Do not dismiss modern hybrids completely, however, because some of them have advantages in terms of quality, productivity and resistance to pests and diseases.

Sowing and planting methods

Vegetables are usually grown from seed. They can be sown outdoors in drills in a permanent site (known as direct sowing) or in a seedbed for transplanting later. They can also be sown under glass in trays or modules for transplanting outdoors. The latter method is suitable for tender crops such as tomatoes, (bell) peppers and aubergines (eggplants), or any that are likely to be a prey to slugs. If you want to avoid the seed-raising stage, many crops can be bought as young plants.

Broadcast sowing is a traditional method of sowing seed in which it is scattered evenly over well-prepared and raked ground. The soil is then lightly raked again to cover the seed. Although quick and simple, it is less used in vegetable gardens because it can be difficult to sow the seed evenly and wastes more seed than sowing in drills. It is, however, useful in informal areas where you want to combine vegetables and flowers, as you can mix together the seeds of carrots and cornflowers (*Centaurea cyanus*), for example, and let them grow up together.

Planting depths and distances

You need to ensure that the plants in your vegetable plot are well spaced out, meaning the distance both between plants in a row and between the rows, to reduce competition for water and nutrients. Each plant has individual spacing requirements, but the informality of a cottage garden means that you can grow vegetables among the flowers, so you don't have to be dogmatic about advised planting distances. Just use them as a general guideline and sow seed or plant out young plants wherever you see a gap in a border.

ABOVE LEFT AND RIGHT: *Productive gardens can be as colourful and easy on the eye as purely ornamental ones.*

SOWING VEGETABLES IN DRILLS

Sowing in straight drills is the most common way to sow vegetable seeds. It looks neat and makes it easier to identify the vegetable seedlings from any weeds that may emerge. Of course, drills do not have to be straight and you can sow in sweeping curves or wavy lines if you prefer. On heavy clay soil, it can help to sprinkle a layer of sand or grit along the drill before sowing the seed.

1 Mark out the drill with a garden line. Use a hoe to make a drill of a suitable depth for the seed being sown.

2 If the soil is dry, then water the drill right along its length.

3 Sprinkle the seeds evenly along the drill – shown here is the turnip 'Scarlet Queen' which can be sown throughout the summer.

4 Carefully cover the seed with the soil. In dry weather, water as necessary to ensure the soil stays reasonably moist.

and beans); group two contains the brassicas (cabbages, broccoli, kale etc.); group three contains onions, lettuce, garlic and sweetcorn; and group four includes root crops and tomatoes.

Treat the soil in each area to suit what is planted there. Root crops prefer an alkaline soil, so add lime and limit manure. Tomatoes like acidic soil, so feed them well and add manure. Legume crops like frequent feeding and will leave the soil nitrogen-rich for the brassicas and leafy greens that follow.

Some crops, including salad crops and perennial plants such as asparagus, globe artichokes and rhubarb, do not form part of the rotation groups. Perennial crops are best grown in a fifth, permanent bed. Salad plants usually mature quickly and so are often used for intercropping – that is the growing of fast-maturing vegetables between slower-growing crops – or to fill temporary gaps between slower crops.

ABOVE: *This corner bed includes curly kale, Hemerocallis 'Stella de Oro', strawberry, globe artichoke, French marigolds, lettuce, fennel, corn and borage.*

Crop rotation

This is the practice of changing the growing position of annual crops each year to avoid the build-up of soil-borne pests and diseases. Specific groups of vegetables are moved around in sequence so that they are not grown in the same area again for at least three years. To use a four-year crop rotation, divide the garden into four areas. Group one contains the legumes (peas

Companion planting

This is the practice of growing plants that may have a beneficial effect on their neighbours by either encouraging pollinating insects or repelling pests. For example, marigolds – particularly the French marigold (*Tagetes patula*) – have been found to repel whitefly and even soil nematodes. They are long-flowering plants and, like nasturtiums (*Tropaeolum majus*), also attract many pollinators.

PLANTING OUT VEGETABLE SEEDLINGS

Seedlings that are raised in modules or small pots develop quickly without competition from others and can be planted out with very little root disturbance. Make sure that they are hardened off to acclimatize them to outdoor conditions before planting them out permanently. Cloches or cold frames are useful at this stage. Those shown here are cabbage seedlings.

1 Remove the seedling from the module – a pencil pushed through the drainage hole will help ease the rootball out.

2 If there is more than one seedling in each module, plant them out together. You can remove the weaker ones later.

3 Make a hole for the rootball with a trowel. Place the plant in the hole so that its lower leaves are level with the soil surface.

4 Firm in and water well. Keep the seedlings evenly moist until they are established.

LEFT: *Aubergines (eggplants), such as the compact cultivar 'Baby Rosanna', are best grown in pots on a warm patio.*

BELOW: *Globe artichokes (*Cynara cardunculus)*, and their close relative the cardoon (C. cardunculus var.* sylvestris)*, are grown as permanent members of a border.*

Harvesting and storage

To avoid gluts or hungry gaps in your harvesting schedule, sow vegetables in succession throughout the season. Wait until one sowing has emerged and then start another one. Many leafy salad vegetables can be harvested as seedling crops and, once cut, may resprout to produce a second or third cut.

Most vegetables are harvested just before they reach full maturity, which gives them a richer flavour. Early harvesting means that the vegetables are sweeter and more tender. New potatoes can be dug as the plants start to flower, but for full-sized maincrop potatoes, wait until the tops of the plants start to die back. Many of the vegetables that are botanically considered as classified fruits, such as cordon tomatoes, courgettes (zucchini) and runner (green) beans, should be picked regularly to encourage the plant to keep producing more.

In areas with severe winters, there is a greater urgency to harvest and store crops before they are damaged by frost. Parsnips, however, often taste better if left in the ground until after a frost or two. Some vegetables such as sweet (bell) peppers, certain cultivars of marrow (large zucchini) and squash and 'Long Keeper'-type tomatoes may be stored for several months in a dry, frost-free environment.

MAINTAINING VEGETABLES

Vegetables vary greatly in the amount of care that they require. Key tasks, such as regular watering, feeding and monitoring for pests and diseases, in a vegetable garden are outlined here.

WEEDING
Tackle emerging weeds by running a sharp hoe over the bed or between individual rows. Remove established weeds by hand and pull annual weeds before they set seed. If a weed is close to your vegetables, then just remove the top.

Weeds in the vegetable patch

WATERING AND FEEDING
Water regularly and thoroughly in the morning during dry periods. Vegetables grown in good, rich soil containing plenty of organic matter require little extra feeding, but some crops benefit from additional fertilizers. Both organic and non-organic types are readily available.

Courgette and cabbage bed

MULCHING
This can reduce water evaporation and help to keep weeds down by reducing the amount of bare soil. Organic mulches, such as composted bark or well-rotted garden compost, also improve soil structure once incorporated by worms. Black plastic or woven mulch matting is excellent for weed control, but less aesthetically pleasing.

Mulching the vegetable bed

PROTECTING SEEDLINGS
Young seedlings are vulnerable to bad weather and a variety of pests, so protect them with a cloche or layer of horticultural fleece in adverse conditions. Also protect them with a tunnel of chicken wire or netting supported by bamboo canes if you have free-range chickens or other animals.

A glasshouse with seedlings

GOOD GARDEN HYGIENE
Strong, healthy plants cope better with pests and diseases, so remove and burn any infected plant material. Do not put such material on a compost heap, however, as this can then become a source of infection to any subsequent crops.

Cucumber mosaic virus

fruit trees & soft fruit

Whether grown in an orchard, trained against a wall or fence, or planted in a tub, a fruit tree or two is essential for the cottage garden. The term 'soft fruit' includes bush fruits such as currants and gooseberries, those like raspberries and blackberries that fruit on canes, and strawberries, which are herbaceous perennials.

ABOVE: *Prunus cerasus 'Morello' is a self-fertile tree that produces a heavy crop of dark red acidic cherries – they are too sour for eating but are ideal for cooking.*

ABOVE RIGHT: *Standard apple trees give useful fruit but also add height to the garden.*

Growing fruit trees

Most fruit trees grow best in a sunny, but sheltered, site. However, cottage gardeners had to make do with what they had and fruit can be grown successfully in less-than-ideal settings. The best fruit tree for a shady situation is the self-fertile cooking cherry 'Morello' (*Prunus cerasus*). If you want to grow fruit trees in pots, choose a pot of around 40cm (16in) in diameter. Terracotta pots are heavier and more stable, but dry out more quickly than plastic ones.

The choice of rootstock controls the tree's rate of growth and ultimate height, the time it takes for it to start bearing fruit and its lifespan. Get advice from a nursery on the appropriate rootstock for your requirements.

Some fruit trees are self-fertile, but in many cases they require one or more other varieties to pollinate them, which will obviously need to be those that flower at the same time. If you have neighbours who grow fruit, their trees may helpfully cross-pollinate with yours. Otherwise, you will have to buy two or more trees in the same pollination group, such as the apples 'Cox's Orange Pippin' and 'Fiesta'. Most good catalogues contain information on pollination.

Having planted your trees, an important requirement is mulching to eliminate competition from weeds. Organic mulches such as well-rotted manure or garden compost are ideal because they also provide a supply of nutrients and help to improve soil structure. However, mulches such as these are easily disturbed by birds and you may find that non-organic mulches like woven fibre matting are more effective. You will also need to provide newly planted trees with a guard to protect against pests such as deer, rabbits and rodents.

Pruning requirements

The aim of pruning is to produce a tree of the desired shape with a strong, balanced framework, to maintain the tree's health and ensure a good supply of fruit. Here are some guidelines, but you'll need to refer to pruning requirements for individual trees.

If you prune trees in late winter then the cuts benefit from a short healing time. Pruning earlier in the winter results in cuts that cannot heal until the spring. Winter pruning is usually carried out on apples, pears, quinces and medlar trees. Prune in the winter for bush and tree type fruits, not for trained cordons and espaliers. The latter are best pruned and trained in the summer. Stone fruits, such as apricots, cherries and plums, are pruned in spring or summer to minimize the risk of silver-leaf infection.

Summer pruning is used to restrict the size and vigour of trained fruit trees such as those grown as cordons or fans. Only trees that bear fruit on spurs rather than at the tips of stems can be grown in this way. Summer pruning restricts vegetative growth and promotes fruiting. It is usually carried out in high summer when the new season's growth is starting to get woody at the base. Any new shoots that are more than

around 20cm (8in) in length, growing from the main structural branches, are cut to three leaves above the cluster of leaves that forms nearest the main branches. Any sub-shoots are cut back hard to just one leaf. Shoots that are less than 20cm (8in) in length are usually left, as they tend to end in a fruit bud.

ABOVE: *Established orchards look best in the spring when the blossom complements daffodil underplanting.*

PLANTING AND STAKING A FRUIT TREE

A newly planted fruit tree will need staking. Some need permanent stakes, either metal posts or wooden ones treated with preservative, but most require a temporary stake. This needs to be inserted well outside of the root circle, and is designed to support the tree as it becomes established, after which it can be removed. Before buying a tree, check that it is on a rootstock that is suitable for your needs.

1 Thoroughly prepare the earth around the hole and in the bottom, adding plenty of well-rotted organic matter. Check that the rootball is not pot-bound. If the roots are tangled, gently tease them out, handling them as little as possible.

2 Place the young tree into the hole and check that the surrounding soil is approximately level with that in the container. You should not put the graft (visible as a bulge in the trunk) below ground.

3 Knock a post in at an angle to avoid damaging the roots. Cut off any extra, so that it does not present a hazard. Firmly secure the tree to the post, using a proper tree tie. Do not use string or anything that can cut into or chafe the trunk.

4 The tree is now ready for its initial pruning. The shape should be rectified at each stage of pruning to ensure that it grows evenly. The ground should be mulched to reduce surrounding weed growth and protect the roots.

RIGHT: *The medlar* (Mespilus germanica) *is an old-fashioned tree that has been around for over 3,000 years. The fruit is hard and acidic and needs to be left on the tree through the first winter frost before it is edible. It has a distinctive aroma and its flavour has been described as "a combination of the tastes of fig, kumquat, loquat and Persian dates".*

Cottage-garden orchards

Traditional cottage-garden orchards are a style apart from commercial ones, where plants are grafted on to dwarfing rootstocks so that the fruit is easy to pick. In contrast, cottage-garden fruit trees may be tall, old and, without rigid staking and pruning, they take on all kinds of shapes.

Existing areas of orchard should be treasured because they may be a sanctuary for local or little-grown cultivars of fruit, and large old trees can still be very productive, but when planting new trees, smaller ones are usually more practical.

Many fruits such as apples have what is called a chilling requirement. For flowering to occur, the fruit trees must be subjected to around 900 hours of temperatures below 7°C (45°F). For this reason, apples do not grow well in tropical areas because they do not receive adequate chilling, and an orange grove may be more appropriate in areas with a warm climate such as Florida in the United States.

PLANTING BLUEBERRIES IN A CONTAINER

Blueberry bushes are best planted during their dormant season, usually in late spring. Select varieties according to their time of ripening: early or mid-season varieties work best in containers. It is useful to have the cross-pollination benefit of at least 2 bushes. *Vaccinium* 'Reveille', 'Sunshine Blue' and 'North Blue' varieties offer you great tasting berries and bushes that are highly ornamental in the autumn.

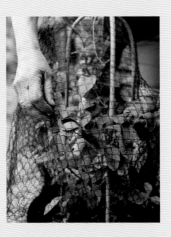

1 Choose a 40–60cm (16–24in) container such as a half barrel and create drainage holes. Place in full sun (blueberries need at least 6 hours of sunlight). Mix the following in equal amounts to fill the container: fine pine bark, peat moss, and prepared ericaceous potting (soil) mix. Use the mixture to fill three-quarters of the container and pack down.

2 Set the bush 2.5–5cm (1–2in) deeper than it was growing in the nursery pot and continue to fill around the root with the mixture. Blueberries are shallow-rooted and like a constantly wet soil, so they need to be watered regularly, always using rainwater, especially during the time of fruit growth through to harvest.

3 Mulch with 5–10cm (2–4in) of sphagnum peat moss to keep the roots cool and moist. Other options are bark mulch, sawdust or grass clippings. Fertilize plants lightly 4 to 6 weeks after planting using a fertilizer for acid-loving plants. Apply one portion around mid-winter, one at the beginning of summer, and the last towards the end of summer.

4 Add a plant support made out of 2 bamboo hoops. Birds love blueberries, so as the blueberries ripen use a bird-proof plastic mesh or very light gauge muslin (cheesecloth). These still allow sun and rain to reach the bushes. In winter, wrap bushes in hessian (burlap) or move them into a sheltered spot to avoid wind and drying damage.

FAR LEFT: *Figs need a warm climate and plenty of sunlight. You need to restrict the roots when planting, if you want them to fruit without growing very large.*

LEFT: *Strawberry plants send out runners over the soil's surface – they can be pegged down and will then form a separate plant.*

BELOW LEFT: *The garden hedge can be highly productive when brambles and hops are allowed to scramble through it.*

BELOW: *White currants* (Ribes sativum) *are less likely to be taken by birds than redcurrants.*

Growing soft fruit

Soft fruits may be planted in a separate area or among ornamental plants. Most soft fruit is attractive to birds and requires some form of protection. Of all fruits it is perhaps the gooseberry that is most closely associated with cottage gardens. Most of the gooseberries sold in supermarkets today are only suitable for cooking, so if you grow the fruits yourself you might choose one of the wide range of dessert gooseberries such as 'Broomgirl' or 'Dan's Mistake'.

Strawberries are another popular soft fruit. Wild strawberries were always valued for their sweetness and intensity of flavour, but it is the hybrid *Fragaria* x *ananassa* that has led to the wide range of cultivars grown today. Particularly good for flavour are 'Cambridge Late Pine', 'Marshmallow', the perpetual-fruiting 'Aromel' and 'Mara des Bois'.

Grow strawberries in a warm, sunny position to give the best-flavoured fruits, rotating the plants to a new area every three years. Provide a regular supply of water, remove excess runners as they develop and keep the bed clear of weeds. As the fruit trusses develop, put a thick layer of straw underneath the fruit to reduce the incidence of fungal diseases. Allow the fruit to ripen fully on the plant before picking to achieve the best flavour. Strawberries can also be grown in hanging baskets or containers, as well as the traditional terracotta strawberry pot.

Currants are as easy to grow as gooseberries, because they are tolerant of a range of soils and either sun or partial shade, although they do better in cool climates. Currants do not have thorns and so are easier to pick. Blackcurrants (*Ribes nigrum*) have an intense flavour and are usually cooked

rather than eaten raw. Remove one-third of the fruited stems each year to stimulate new growth. Red and white currants are colour variants of *Ribes sativum*. They can be grown as open bushes or trained as cordons or fans.

Blueberries (*Vaccinium*) can also be a satisfying crop if you have an acid soil. The bushes are very attractive with pretty, white, bell-like flowers and the leaves have a good autumn colour. If you have an alkaline soil, blueberries can be grown in tubs of ericaceous potting (soil) mix.

One of the easiest soft fruits to grow is rhubarb (*Rheum x hybridum*) which, if provided with a fertile soil in sun or shade, will produce succulent stems for many years.

the potager garden

The geometric beds of a potager are often laid out in carefully planned, symmetrical patterns, giving a sense of formality. While a potager garden has a clearly defined sense of order and cottage-garden plantings are more random, the two approaches both combine edible and ornamental plants.

TOP: *The Italian kale (Brassica oleracea var. acephala 'Nero di Toscana') has narrow, deep green leaves that contrast well with lighter shades.*

ABOVE: *The rich colours of cabbage leaves (Brassica oleracea) make an effective foil to these vibrant late-summer Dahlia 'Bishop of Llandaff'.*

OPPOSITE: *Trained fruit trees and standard roses add height to this colourful potager.*

Designing a cottage potager

The term 'potager', used to describe a kitchen garden, arose from the French *jardin potager*, meaning a garden that provides vegetables for the pot. It usually refers to a kitchen garden in which the vegetables are selected for their ornamental qualities and which is laid out in a decorative, often geometric, pattern. The colours and patterns of a potager form is an attractive structure for a modern cottage-style kitchen garden, and the mixture of edible produce and ornamental plants gives extra charm and animation.

The most famous potager, the Potager du Roi at Versailles, France, has a 3 hectare (7.5 acre) main square that is divided into 16 smaller squares with different vegetable varieties. However, potagers can be designed on a much smaller scale. The essential ingredients are neatly laid-out beds with a selection of decorative vegetables and a mixture of flowers and herbs. The beds may be laid out in any way, a square chequerboard pattern being common. Having a few large beds is more practical than many small ones, but do not make them wider than 1.2m (4ft), so that you can tend the plants without stepping on the beds.

The paths between the beds can be made from beaten earth or gravel, although brick paths look better and are easier to walk on in wet weather. Include a focal point such as an arch or cast-iron, obelisk-type support, over which you can train cordon tomatoes or garden beans. Hazel or willow rods can be used to create teepees for beans or sweet peas (*Lathyrus odoratus*) to scramble up. Alternatively, a bench, sundial or tall strawberry pot could be used. Even architectural plants such as the globe artichoke in the red-flowered form, *Cynara cardunculus* Scolymus Group 'Concerto', can provide a focal point. Hoops made from iron or brushwood might be installed over the paths for gourds or nasturtiums (*Tropaeolum majus*) to climb over, providing colour and interest through to autumn.

The beds in many potagers are edged with low box hedging, using the dwarf cultivar *Buxus sempervirens* 'Suffruticosa'. Box plants, however, are prone to box blight, a serious leaf disease. The symptoms are dark brown spots on the leaves, which eventually cover the whole leaf and cause defoliation. If the disease is present in your area, plant *Buxus microphylla* 'Faulkner', which is more resistant to the disease, a dwarf hebe such as *Hebe pinguifolia* 'Sutherlandii', or hyssop (*Hyssopus officinalis*).

Simple edgings can be formed from rows of dwarf marigolds (*Tagetes*), alpine strawberries or ribbons of parsley (*Petroselinum crispum*). Step-over apple trees or trained cane fruits also make ideal edgings for beds. Edging plants will compete with the vegetables for water and nutrients, and for this reason, many people prefer to use tiles or wooden boards.

Choosing plants for a potager

Within the beds, the seed of salad plants can be sown in neat blocks or waves, zigzags or triangles. Coloured-leaved plants, such as the beetroot 'Bull's Blood' and the lettuce 'Red Sails', usually have more impact when planted in blocks. Other attractive vegetables include Swiss chard, Tuscan kale, corn, red cabbages and feathery-leaved carrots. Include plenty of plants with edible flowers such as nasturtiums, borage (*Borago officinalis*), chives (*Allium schoenoprasum*), sweet violets (*Viola odorata*) and pinks (*Dianthus plumarius*). Sow a succession of plants in pots or modules, so that you have more plants to fill in gaps as you harvest the produce.

livestock & wildlife

Livestock in the early cottage gardens was at least as important as edible crops. Rearing animals such as sheep and cows is a rarity today, but many gardeners can find space for smaller livestock such as chickens and ducks, or even a pig or goat. As well as a ready supply of eggs, milk or meat, they will provide animal manure to enrich the garden, while grazing animals such as geese and sheep will keep meadow and orchard areas under control.

With wildlife under pressure from loss of habitats or changes in farming practices, gardens have become a haven for many birds and other wild creatures. Encouraging them therefore helps to conserve the rich diversity of the natural world. Dense and varied plantings of old-fashioned flowers, rich in nectar and pollen, make the garden a magnet for wildlife. Providing food, shelter and secure nesting sites will entice more creatures, and we can enjoy watching them and listening to the sounds of bees and birds.

LEFT: *A bee feeding on lavender blossom.* ABOVE LEFT: *The European hedgehog (Erinaceus europaeus) is a popular garden visitor as it eats slugs and other pests.* ABOVE CENTRE: *Apart from being great characters, domestic geese will supply delicious eggs, keep lawns under control and are effective burglar alarms.* ABOVE RIGHT: *A handful of day-old Egyptian Fayoumi chicks.*

keeping chickens

Chickens are generally very easy to keep, but looking after them is a responsibility and so you need to understand their requirements before taking them on. You should also check with your local authority and in the deeds of your property to make sure that there are no restrictions on keeping livestock.

ABOVE: *A Sultan hen keeps a careful watch over her chicks.*

RIGHT: *'Buff Orpington' hens have free range of the garden, with protection provided for border plants. Heavy breeds often do less damage than lighter, more active foragers.*

FAR RIGHT: *This young Appenzeller cockerel is an active bird that would happily roost in a tree in the orchard if permitted.*

OPPOSITE: *This Blue Cochin hen proudly watches over her foster chicks, including Araucanas, Sultans and Penedesencas.*

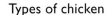

Types of chicken

Various factors will influence your decision on what chickens to keep. Many hybrid birds such as Black Rocks lay well all year round and so are ideal if you want maximum egg production, while some breeds were specifically developed for meat production. Most breeds of chicken are available as large fowl or as bantam/miniature versions. Large fowl are better if you want good-sized eggs or meat birds, but bantams are more suitable for a small garden and for children to handle. If there is a poultry club in your area, attend one of the shows to find out about the different kinds of birds that are available. Many people prefer to keep birds that were developed in their area because they are better adapted to local conditions. This also helps in the conservation of local chicken breeds.

For rich brown eggs, try the French Maran, a big bird usually seen in mottled, cuckoo colours, or the Penedesenca, a rare breed from the Catalan region of Spain. Araucana chickens, which come from northern Chile, lay lovely, clear blue eggs. The birds usually have a small crest, a feathery beard and tufts of feathers growing outward from the sides of the head. The Buckeye from Ohio in the United States is mainly kept for meat production, but also lays brown eggs and has beautiful, chestnut-brown plumage. The Rhode Island Red and the Jersey Giant are both popular North American breeds and are good layers.

One of the most ornamental of chicken breeds is the Sultan, a beautiful bird that used to strut around the palace gardens in what is now Turkey. It is a profusely feathered breed, generally seen in pure white, with a rounded crest, beard and feathery legs and feet. Like the Poland, another crested breed, it does best in dry climates or with a covered run because it quickly becomes bedraggled in wet weather.

A popular bantam type that is suitable for children is the Pekin. These birds are round and fluffy, come in many colours and are extremely docile.

The hen house

Chickens need a hen house to provide shelter from inclement weather and security from predators. Small, movable units with an attached run are popular because they can be transferred to fresh ground on a regular basis. Garden sheds and unwanted playhouses can often be converted for use by chickens, but make sure that there is adequate ventilation and easy access, both for the birds and for cleaning out. Housing that is lifted off the ground will prevent rats from nesting underneath. Provide plenty of perches, as the birds will feel safer if they can roost off the floor at night. Nest boxes should be in the darkest part of the house. If you keep several chickens, allow at least one box for every four hens.

If you buy second-hand poultry housing, spray it against mites, which are able to live in housing for several months after the original birds have been removed. There are various organic mite-repellent powders available. Alternatively, you can pass a blowtorch over the inside of the house to kill off the mites. Avoid hen houses covered with roofing felt, however, because the mites like to creep into the space between the wood and the felt.

Even if you give your birds free range, it is advisable to install a run on well-drained soil for the hen house. Placing old pallets on top of the mud is a good temporary solution if the land becomes waterlogged. Also make sure that the run is secure from foxes. If you have a permanent run, bury the mesh in the ground, folding it out for a distance of approximately 30cm (12in) to prevent foxes digging underneath it. The best mesh to use is a heavy-gauge, welded mesh because this also keeps out wild birds and rodents. For large runs, electric fencing is the best option, with solar panels to keep the batteries topped up.

RIGHT: *Keeping chickens is not really time-consuming but you must be prepared to clean out the houses regularly and provide fresh straw.*

BELOW: *Chickens are happiest if they are allowed to range freely in the garden.*

Cleaning out a hen house

The first stage is to line the main hen house and any attached nest boxes with newspaper. Add a deep layer of clean softwood shavings or straw. Do not use hay because even good-quality hay may contain mould pores that can cause respiratory problems. At weekly intervals, simply remove the newspaper, straw and accumulated droppings, and add to the compost heap. Around once a month, clean the hen house more thoroughly by scrubbing any perches or using a pressure washer to remove dried-on droppings.

Feeding chickens

Free-range chickens will find most of their own food, eating a variety of vegetation and insects. However, giving them a handful of feed per bird, both morning and evening, will ensure that they receive a balanced diet. Supplies of feed must be kept in a vermin-proof bin. Chickens' food and water should be kept in a covered area in order to keep out rain and reduce the risk of contamination by wild birds.

The simplest choice of feed is to use a proprietary brand formulated for the growth stage of your birds. Young birds from 6 to 20 weeks of age are usually fed grower's pellets. Most breeds are ready to start laying eggs at between 18 and 21 weeks, at which time they are fed layers' pellets. If you plan to let your birds breed, there are special

breeder's rations available. Mixed corn should not be given as the main food source because it may not provide enough protein, but it is useful as a supplementary food.

All birds need a supply of insoluble grit such as flint or granite, which helps digestion, so provide this on an ad-hoc basis. Adding crushed oyster shells to the chicken's diet provides valuable calcium – this strengthens the shells of the chickens' eggs, which can be soft or thin without this addition.

A constant supply of fresh drinking water is essential. Birds with clean water on demand will be larger, stronger, healthier and better layers than those with a more limited water supply.

Egg-laying

If you are planning to rear your own chicks then you need fertile eggs and therefore must have a cockerel. One cockerel will serve several females. If you have more than one cockerel, keep them separately as they are likely to fight.

Chickens normally live for 7 to 10 years, although some may live longer. Egg production is usually at its peak in the birds' second year and then slows down with age. Hens lay eggs whether or not there is a cockerel around, so there is no need to have a cockerel if you do not want the eggs to hatch. Cockerels are usually very handsome birds and assiduous in finding food for their hens, but they are also noisy and can be aggressive, particularly in the breeding season.

To produce eggs actively, hens need about 14 hours of light each day so it can be wise to add supplemental light to the coop in the winter. Other factors that affect productivity are lack of protein or calcium in the diet or overheated hens.

Collecting eggs

Hens usually lay their eggs in the morning. Collect the eggs every day. Do not wash the eggs, however, because this can cause bacteria to penetrate the porous shell. Wipe the eggs with a clean cloth if they are badly soiled. Store the eggs in a refrigerator, preferably in an egg tray away from other foods.

LEFT: *You may wish to keep hens in a fenced-off part of the garden rather than giving them total freedom.*

BELOW: *Even very young children will enjoy feeding the chickens.*

BELOW LEFT: *Collecting eggs is another daily task that children will take great pleasure in.*

NATURAL INCUBATION

While many chicken owners use artificial incubation and a controlled indoor environment to hatch their chickens' eggs, the most natural way is to allow a broody hen to do the work. Hens of many modern, egg-laying breeds are rarely broody, while those that are can be unreliable sitters. Older breeds, such as cochins and silkies, regularly go broody and make good mothers. Broody chickens sit tight on the nest, rarely leaving to eat or drink, and protest vigorously if removed.

1 Set the broody hen in a quiet, secure place such as a special broody ark or a cardboard box lined with straw in a corner of the potting shed.

2 While brooding, the hen will keep the eggs at a constant temperature and humidity, as well as turn them regularly. Ensure that she leaves the eggs once a day to eat, drink and defecate.

3 Chicks hatch after about 21 days. Bantams may take a day or two less and large fowl slightly longer. The hen usually stays on the nest for about two days after the first egg has hatched.

4 After a couple of days, the hen will take her chicks outside. Give them proprietary chick crumbs and fresh water in a shallow bowl containing pebbles so that the chicks do not drown.

General care

Chickens are usually healthy birds, but they are prone to various parasites, so handle them regularly and inspect them for lice and mites. Pests are most likely to be seen around the vent region (rear end) of the bird or the head of crested birds. Chickens need to be wormed on a regular basis, so check with your local veterinary surgeon for up-to-date advice.

You should also note that chickens experience an annual moult in which they replace all their feathers. Although the process is gradual, it sometimes occurs more rapidly and can look alarming. Feathers are around 85% protein, so it is important that the birds are fed a good-quality diet at this time.

Nesting and hatching eggs

Although you can buy chickens at any age, from day-old chicks to mature egg-laying hens, there are many advantages to hatching chickens yourself. It is certainly cheaper to buy fertile eggs than mature hens. Eggs usually survive the postal system well, so you will not have to travel long distances to obtain stock of rare breeds. There is also less chance that you will inadvertently introduce parasites or diseases into your flock.

However, unless you are hatching eggs from your own chickens or know the egg supplier well, you have to trust that the eggs come from quality stock and, of course, the proportion of hens to cocks that you will hatch is always a gamble. If you have your own broody hen she will do the work of hatching the eggs for you. Alternatively, you may choose to use an incubator.

ABOVE: LEFT: *Cochin eggs are smaller than you would expect for the size of the bird.*

ABOVE: *A young Nankin bantam chick exploring.*

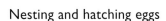

Artifical incubation

If you do not have a suitable broody hen, then you can hatch eggs with an artificial incubator. This gives you the opportunity to watch the eggs hatch and rear any resulting chicks by hand, which are then usually very tame and trusting.

If you don't want to use your own chickens' eggs, fertile eggs can be ordered from hatcheries or poultry farmers who have roosters. You need to have an artificial incubator, set up according to the manufacturer's instructions, and allow it to run for several hours. Double-check the temperature (37.5°C/99°F) and humidity levels (40–50 per cent), and then set your eggs. Record the date set on a calendar. If the incubator does not have automatic turning, you will need to turn the eggs manually about four times a day. Check water levels every day or so. Stop turning the eggs and increase the humidity to 60 to 70 per cent around three days before the chicks are due to hatch. Resist the temptation to take off the lid of the incubator because this reduces humidity levels and can make hatching more difficult. The eggs will begin to hatch on day 21 (sometimes sooner for bantams). Any eggs that have not hatched by day 25 should be removed and discarded.

LEFT: *Incubators are available in many sizes, depending on how many eggs you want to hatch. More sophisticated models will turn the eggs as well as control the humidity.*

LOOKING AFTER YOUR CHICKS AS THEY GROW

While the eggs are incubating make sure that you are prepared to look after the chicks once they hatch. Newly hatched chicks have enough resources to last for the first 24–48 hours but can be offered a proprietary chick feed and water as soon as they are dried off and running around. They must be kept warm at around 32°C (90°F). Make sure that any predators such as domestic cats cannot reach them. Wait for the chicks to reach 4–6 weeks old before moving them outside to a permanent sheltered, predator-proof enclosure.

1 (30 minutes old). It is normal for chicks to hatch within a 24-hour period. After hatching, the chicks should remain in the incubator for 24 hours to allow them to dry out and fluff up.

2 (3 days old) Transfer the chicks to a prepared brooding area such as a cardboard box with a heat lamp above it. Use an old towel or newspaper to cover the base so that the chicks don't slip.

3 (5 days old). Feed the chicks with a proprietary chick crumb and provide fresh water in a shallow bowl containing pebbles or marbles so that they do not drown.

4 (19 days old). Start to gradually reduce the temperature of their housing and accustom them to normal outdoor temperatures. By three weeks old you will see the growth of adult feathers.

ducks & geese
Ducks are wonderfully comical creatures of great character. They can be reared for their eggs, meat and down, used as slug-control officers or simply kept for fun. Geese are bigger than ducks and produce really good-sized tasty eggs. They spend a lot of time grazing and make useful lawnmowers, but can be messy and noisy.

Types of duck

The rearing of ducks, such as the white Aylesbury duck, was a typical cottage industry in parts of England from the late 17th century. The cottagers bought fertile eggs and hatched them using broody hens. The ducklings were initially reared inside the cottages for warmth and security from predators, often resulting in squalid conditions in the home.

Today you can keep wild-species waterfowl or choose from different breeds of domesticated ducks and geese. Aylesbury ducks are kept mostly as exhibition birds. Indian runner ducks, which have a characteristically upright stance, are popular and quite good egg layers. The crested Indian runner, known as the Bali duck, is particularly ornamental. Most domestic ducks have the wild mallard as an ancestor; the muscovy, however, originates in South and Central America. Muscovies make good pets and have an endearing way of greeting you with a nodding head and wagging tail. They are good at catching flies, ticks and other pests.

Types of geese

Geese range in size, from the light Shetland breed from the north of Scotland up to heavyweights such as the French Toulouse breed, which was developed for the production of foie gras. The most ornamental of the goose breeds is the Sebastopol, which originated in South-eastern Europe. They have wonderful, long, curly feathers that can be four times the length of those found in other breeds. Geese are very effective guards, although the noise they make on seeing anyone new may disturb any close neighbours.

ABOVE LEFT: *Goslings such as these Sebastopols are cute, and if handled regularly usually remain tame.*

LEFT: *Muscovy ducks, like this drake, are intelligent birds and make good pets.*

BELOW LEFT: *There are many breeds of domestic geese – Chinese geese have a distinctive knob on their bills.*

BELOW: *Ducks need a secure house to protect them from predators who may threaten them in the night.*

TOP LEFT: *These newly hatched ducklings and goslings spend the night in a propagator – their water bowl has marbles added so they don't drown.*

MIDDLE: *If they have no access to a pond, ducks need a bath that is large enough to bathe in.*

TOP RIGHT: *Ducks will help to keep the garden free of slugs and snails.*

FAR LEFT BOTTOM: *House goslings in a secure pen so they are able to graze outdoors safely.*

Taking care of ducks and geese

Ducks do not require much attention. They happily forage for most of their own food, although they are usually fed a handful of poultry layer's pellets in the morning and a handful of wheat in the evening. They need fresh drinking water daily. Unlike ducks and chickens, geese are predominantly grazing animals and so they require little in the way of extra feed if you have suitable grassy areas. They are ideal for clearing up windfall apples in an orchard. Ducks and geese are not particularly prone to pests and diseases, although they need regular worming. Do not allow them access to poisonous plants such as daphnes and nightshades (*Solanum* spp.).

A spacious pond is not necessary for keeping ducks and geese, but if you have a garden pond, then they will enjoy it. However, in order to keep their feathers in good condition, they require a bath that is large enough for them to immerse their heads. They also need a secure house in which you can shut them at night to keep them safe from predators such as foxes. The house must be well ventilated, but it does not need separate nesting boxes because ducks lay their eggs on the floor.

If you want to hatch eggs, use a broody hen or duck or an artificial incubator, as with chickens. Duck eggs take 28 days to hatch and goose eggs 30 days. They require a higher relative humidity than chicken eggs.

HOLDING A DUCK

It is important that you handle your livestock regularly so that they are accustomed to it, then if they are ill and have to be handled by a veterinary surgeon it is not such a traumatic experience for them.

1 Tame ducks can usually be held easily by holding them against your body, with a hand under their chest to give support.

2 Uncooperative ducks are best held with a hand around the wings at the 'shoulders', because these are the strongest joints.

other animals

For hundreds of years, even the smallest cottage garden would have been home to a pig, which was the staple of the cottage economy, providing food for the family and manure for the garden. If you have a suitable garden, other animals such as goats, sheep, donkeys and even alpacas can also be kept.

TOP: *Dairy goats will provide a plentiful supply of milk for the whiole family.*

ABOVE: *Sturdy fencing is required to keep goats away from your vegetable garden and any ornamental plants.*

ABOVE RIGHT: *This young kid is enjoying itself browsing on garden plants.*

Assess the options

Choosing a rare breed allows you to play your part in the conservation of breeds that may not be suitable for modern commercial farming. Visit agricultural shows and talk to breeders before making any decisions. Also, make sure that you can comply with any animal health legislation. Details vary from country to country, so you should enquire at your local Department of Agriculture or equivalent body.

Goats

One of the first animals to be domesticated, goats are charming creatures with great character and are ideal for spacious cottage gardens. Not only do they provide a useful source of milk and meat, but they also have an acute sense of curiosity and can be very affectionate. There are over 300 breeds of goat to choose from. It is advisable to buy pedigree stock registered with your National Society.

The Anglo Nubian goat of Middle Eastern origin is a large, heavy breed with a striking Roman nose and pendulous ears. Its milk has a high protein and butterfat content and is good for cheese-making. Golden Guernseys, small animals with a gentle disposition and a steady yield of milk, are also popular. Angoras are kept primarily for the wool called mohair which has very long, lustrous fibres.

Goats are sociable animals and must not be kept alone. Male goats have a pungent odour and are usually kept only by serious breeders. Excess males can be used for their meat, which is low in cholesterol. Goats require robust fencing that is at least 1.2m (4ft) high. Ideally, a pair of goats should be kept on 1/8 hectare (1/3 acre) of land. An area of orchard is perfect because the trees provide shade from hot sun, but you will need to protect the bark from browsing. If less land is available or the grazing is poor, the goats will need supplementary feeding. They require a diet of hay, grass/forage and a specific goat concentrate, which is usually composed of mixed cereals with high-protein foods such as soya meal and crushed peas.

Provide a dry, draught-free shelter with good ventilation and sufficient headroom, allowing at least 3–4 sq m (32–43 sq ft) of floor space per goat. A sturdy hayrack is necessary at goat-head height and a bench for kids to jump on and off. Food and water buckets must be firmly secured.

Pigs

As well as grazing, pigs will eat entire plants, worms, beetles and small rodents. Interesting pig breeds include the Tamworth, a boisterous breed that has a ginger coat and pricked ears. The Oxford Sandy and Black, with a ginger coat with black spots, is a traditional cottager's pig that is both hardy and docile. The Gloucestershire Old Spot was traditionally kept in orchards and reared on windfall apples. The Duroc is a deep red-coated pig from the United States. It has a deep, muscular body and is much prized for its meat. The Large Black, a docile breed with appealing lop ears, is ideal for keeping in the open because its colour helps it to resist sunburn. The curly coated Mangalitza from central Europe has meat that is high in fat and is popular for making salami.

Sheep

Many people keep sheep to mow grassy areas instead of using machinery. Breeds have been developed for specific purposes such as wool, meat or milk production or to suit particular climates. Smaller breeds, such as the Hebridean,

Ryeland, Shetland and Soay, are probably best for orchards as they are less likely to strip leaves and fruit from the trees. In the United States, miniature sheep, developed mostly from the Welsh Brecknock Cheviot, are becoming popular as pets.

Donkeys

These animals should not be seen just as ornamental additions to a paddock or orchard. They are happier and healthier if they are kept busy carrying reasonable loads of wood or compost around the garden or transporting small children on a family picnic. They are highly intelligent animals and require companionship, ideally of their own kind, although they will also befriend horses or goats. They need a minimum of 1/5 hectare (1/2 acre) of land per animal, as well as a shelter to protect them from bad weather. Donkeys need regular hoof trimming and inoculations against both equine influenza and tetanus.

Alpacas, llamas and guanacos

All camelid animals, including alpacas, llamas and guanacos, produce high-quality fleeces, with fine fibres that do not contain lanolin, making them suitable for those allergic to sheep's wool. They are endearing animals with a lovely, placid nature and are easy to care for. Up to six alpacas can be kept on 1 acre (1/2 hectare) of land with a shelter to provide protection from very wet weather. They must not be kept singly because this can cause them distress. Males will protect their flock against predators such as foxes, and are sometimes kept to protect chickens and other poultry.

BELOW LEFT: *Young alpacas, known as crias, are usually weaned from their mother at six months of age.*

BELOW CENTRE: *Before you buy any pigs contact your local Department of Agriculture for advice.*

BELOW: *Donkeys are intelligent and make lovely family pets.*

beekeeping
In the past, honey was valued as a natural sweetener and used fermented to produce the alcoholic drink mead. Beeswax was also an important product, used as a base for paint, as well as in polishes, cosmetics and candles. Bees would therefore have been an invaluable practical addition to the cottage garden.

ABOVE: *Honey bees should be kept in movable frame hives to allow for regular inspection of the colony.*

BELOW: *Beehives will benefit from an organic kitchen garden with flowers for nectar and no pesticides used.*

BELOW RIGHT: *Protective clothing is required in order to minimize the number of stings.*

Types of beehive
The traditional cottage-garden hive was a hollowed-out log, simple wooden box or rounded skep, a lightweight straw basket, which was bound with natural fibres and often coated with a layer of fresh cow dung to improve weather resistance. A hackle, shaped like an inverted ice-cream cone and made from bundles of straw that were lashed together, provided further protection. Skeps are still sometimes made by beekeepers today because they find them convenient to use when catching swarms, but they are not permitted for standard use in many countries.

The problem with skeps and similar methods is that harvesting the honey involves breaking up the whole comb and, usually, the destruction of the colony. The invention of the top-opening, movable comb hive by Lorenzo Lorraine Langstroth (1810–1895) revolutionized beekeeping. Langstroth

designed a series of wooden frames that fit within a box, with a 'bee space' of 5–8mm (¼–⅜in) between the frames. The bees build parallel honeycombs on the frames without bonding them. This means that the beekeeper can remove individual frames for inspection or harvesting without disturbing the colony. This hive is still used in the United States today.

In Great Britain, the most common type is the British National Hive. Hives are usually made of wood, but polystyrene (Styrofoam) ones are also available (although these cannot be flamed in the same way if there is an outbreak of disease). Top bar hives, based on a traditional design, are becoming more popular with hobbyist beekeepers. They are cheaper to buy and lighter to work with, but they do not have frames and the filled comb is not returned to the hive after honey extraction, resulting in reduced honey production compared with a movable frame hive.

Getting started

Anyone interested in keeping bees is advised to make contact with their local beekeeping association first. Most beekeeping groups run courses or allow beginners to visit members' hives to experience working with a colony. They will also be able to advise on suitable protective clothing, which should include a tunic with elasticated cuffs to the sleeves, a detachable hat and veil, and a pair of gloves. Honey bees rarely sting unless provoked, but it is best to position hives in an area of garden that is little used to be on the safe side. An ideal location is close to a high boundary fence or hedge because this encourages the bees to fly above head level.

Bees and their care

A healthy honey bee colony can contain as many as 50,000 bees. The queen can lay over 2,000 eggs each day. There will be several hundred drone bees, which are males whose main role is to fertilize young queens. The rest of the colony consists of female worker bees that look after the larvae, construct the honeycomb and forage for nectar, pollen and water.

Bees vary in temperament, foraging ability and resistance to disease, so ask for advice from an experienced keeper or your local Bee Diseases Inspector before you choose them. Obtain your bees from a local supplier because they should then be adapted to your climate. There are two rare bee diseases that you should be aware of: European Foul Brood and American Foul Brood. Varroa mites are an increasing problem and must be monitored and treated as necessary (look out for brown or reddish spots on the white larvae or deformed newly emerged bees).

Keep an eye out for infestations of waxmoths (*Galleria mellonella* and *Achroia grisella*), which lay their eggs in beehives. The larvae feed on comb wax and can destroy old combs.

ABOVE: *Site your hives in a shady position so the bees do not overheat.*

FAR LEFT: *Before the era of wooden hives, straw skeps were common – while basic, they are still used by beekeepers.*

LEFT: *A bee collecting pollen from a purpletop vervain flower (Verbena bonariensis).*

birds

Perhaps the most captivating of visitors, birds bring movement and colour to the cottage garden, as well as a joyful range of chirps and songs. To encourage a greater variety of birds to visit, think carefully about what your garden can offer in terms of food, water and safe places for your flying visitors to roost and nest.

ABOVE: *A basic platform bird table is the best design and is easy to keep clean.*

RIGHT: *Providing a range of bird feeders will encourage many different species to visit the garden.*

FAR RIGHT: *White doves are quiet, unobtrusive creatures to keep in the garden – the most common types are fantails and white homing pigeons.*

OPPOSITE LEFT: *Garden birds will welcome the provision of food throughout the winter when natural food supplies are scarce.*

Attracting birds to your garden

Birds feed on a range of different insects, aphids and caterpillars, so try to avoid using pesticides as much as possible to encourage birds to visit your garden. You can then rely on the visiting birds to control the pests. Grow plants that provide food for birds, including those with berries, like cotoneaster, pyracantha and holly, and those with seeds such as teasels and the shrubby orache (*Atriplex halimus*). It is often assumed that only the hummingbirds of the Americas, the sunbirds of Africa and the honeyeaters of Australia feed on nectar, but blue tits in northern Europe have been seen taking nectar from the flowers of crown imperials (*Fritillaria imperialis*). Plants that are visited by nectar-feeding birds often have red or orange, tubular flowers and include fuchsias, columbines (*Aquilegia*), monardas, penstemons and *Isoplexis canariensis*.

If you provide supplementary food on a bird table or in bird feeders, position them in an open site so that the birds can watch for predators. Do not put out too much food at a time as this can encourage vermin. Consider hygiene at bird-feeding stations also, because fungi will grow on left-over damp seed or debris, and disease can be spread through accumulated droppings. Regularly clean feeders in a bucket of warm, soapy water, using a round-headed brush to dislodge debris. Rinse well to remove traces of soap and allow to dry before refilling.

Providing nesting sites

Climbers against a wall and thick, thorny hedges provide safe places for birds to shelter and nest. Common ivy (*Hedera helix*) is a particularly beneficial plant as it provides year-round cover, late flowers that attract many insects, and berries that ripen in mid-winter. Some birds such as swallows, house martins and American robins use buildings to support their nests and simply require a source of mud to make the nests. A shallow-edged pond with muddy banks is ideal, but any accessible area of bare soil may be used. Potting sheds and other outbuildings also make popular nesting sites.

Providing water

A supply of fresh water for drinking and bathing is important, particularly in times of drought or in hard winters when other sources of water may be frozen. If you do not have a pond, consider providing a birdbath – even an inverted dustbin lid or a similar receptacle is ideal. Change the water regularly and clean the bath with a soft brush, paying particular attention to the removal of algae. Solar-powered, heated birdbaths are available to ensure the water remains ice-free in cold climates.

Helping nesting birds

Birds line their nests with a great variety of materials, from thistledown, dry leaves and mosses to spider webs and animal hair. You can assist them in this task by providing a selection of different materials for their use. If you have pet animals or livestock such as ponies or donkeys, any hair collected when you are grooming will be welcomed by your feathered visitors. Simply fill string bags or plastic net bags, such as those used to hang peanuts out for birds, with some good-sized bundles of hair. Then you can just hang the bags of hair from the branches of a tree or from a bird table.

TIPS ON FEEDING BIRDS

Offer a variety of different foodstuffs in order to attract a range of birds to the garden. If you have problems with squirrels plundering all the food you put out for birds, you may want to consider getting a special feed dispenser with a 'baffle' type collar so that squirrels cannot reach it.

WHAT TO FEED BIRDS

- Peanuts – these are one of the most popular supplementary foods, being high in oils and protein. However, there have been concerns about the quality of some peanuts, which have been found to contain aflatoxin, a poison produced by the fungus *Aspergillus flavus*. Buy peanuts from a reputable supplier and don't use any that show signs of mould.
- Black sunflower seed – any sunflower seeds will attract birds, but the black ones have thinner shells and are a favourite with tits and greenfinches. Sunflower hearts are more expensive, but the birds don't leave husks on the ground. Use the seed all year as they are safe to be fed to young in the nest.
- Niger seed – sometimes called nyjer seed, these very small, black seeds require a special dispenser. They are rich in oil and very popular with goldfinches.

FOODS TO AVOID

- Do not put out foods with a high salt content such as salted peanuts, bacon rind or cheese.
- Avoid anything that may swell up inside the bird, such as desiccated coconut and uncooked rice.
- Any mouldy or spoiled food should be thrown away and not fed to birds.
- Cooking fats from roasting tins should not be given as the juices blend with the fats, and if smeared on feathers can damage their waterproofing ability. They also act as a breeding ground for bacteria.

*The common starling (*Sturnus vulgaris*) is a gregarious bird, but unfortunately in decline.*

*European robins (*Erithacus rubecula*) are usually tame and trusting garden visitors.*

butterflies & bees

It is hard to imagine a cottage garden in the summer without the gentle hum of bees (often the first insects to be seen in late winter and early spring) or butterflies dancing between the flowers. Catering for insects brings an extra dimension to our surroundings and is fundamental for a healthy garden ecosystem.

ABOVE: *The honey bee* (Apis mellifera) *is an important pollinator of many of our food crops.*

BELOW: *The melancholy thistle (*Cirsium heterophyllum)*, like other thistles, is very attractive to insects.*

BELOW RIGHT: *Feeders holding soft fruits will encourage butterflies such as Red Admirals (*Vanessa atalanta*) to visit the garden.*

Attracting butterflies

A suburban garden may attract many species of butterfly and moth over a year. Butterflies enjoy warmth and shelter, so plant nectar-rich flowers in sunny areas and provide large, flat stones for them to bask on. Good nectar plants include many umbelliferous plants like angelica, fennel (*Foeniculum vulgare*) and dill (*Anethum graveolens*). Other herbs such as thyme (*Thymus*), hyssop (*Hyssopus officinalis*) and oregano (*Origanum vulgare*) are also popular. Also leave a few windfall fruits on the ground in autumn to provide food for late-emerging butterflies. A few species of butterfly, such as the peacock (*Inachis io*) and the small tortoiseshell (*Aglais urticae*), hibernate over winter and are often found in sheds and garages.

You can also boost butterfly populations by providing food plants for the caterpillars. Traditional cottage-garden plants, such as the dame's violet (*Hesperis matronalis*), are used by many butterfly species, including the orange tip butterfly, which is also fond of the cuckoo flower (*Cardamine pratensis*). Holly (*Ilex*) and ivy (*Hedera*) plants are visited by the dainty holly blue (*Celastrina argiolus*), while the yellow brimstone butterfly (*Gonepteryx rhamni*) will travel as far as 24km (15 miles) in search of buckthorn (*Rhamnus cathartica*) or alder buckthorn (*Frangula alnus*) on which to lay its eggs.

Attracting moths

Moths are closely related to butterflies and come in a huge variety of shapes, sizes and colours. They are an essential part of the food chain for many birds, bats and mammals. Most moths feed in a similar way to butterflies, but they generally visit flowers at night and are attracted to plants with an evening fragrance. The goat willow (*Salix caprea*) is important for providing nectar early in the season. Good food plants for moth caterpillars include berberis, brambles (*Rubus fruticosus*), dandelions (*Taraxacum*), hawthorns (*Crataegus*) and hazel (*Corylus avellana*).

Attracting bees

Around a third of the human diet is based on insect-pollinated plants, with the honey bee (*Apis mellifera*) being responsible for some 80 per cent of this pollination activity. For this reason, recent dramatic declines in wild bee populations in many parts of the world should be of great concern to us all. Bee-friendly gardens avoid the use of pesticides, particularly systemic insecticides that are absorbed by the plant, because these can pass into the nectar and poison both the adult bees and their larvae.

Grow a range of flowers to attract different species of bee. Bees feed on both nectar, which contains energy in the form of sugars, and pollen, a rich source of oils and protein. Bees also need a supply of water, which they use to help cool the colony in hot weather. In general, those bees with a comparatively short tongue, such as the buff-tailed bumble-bee (*Bombus terrestris*), tend to forage on open flowers, such as asters, coreopsis and cosmos, clover (*Trifolium*), scabious (*Scabiosa*) or plants such as the foxglove (*Digitalis purpurea*) whose open flowers are just the right size for the bee to enter. The bee species *Bombus hortorum*, which is widespread in Europe, has a long tongue and forages on flowers such as columbines (*Aquilegia*), delphiniums and honeysuckle (*Lonicera*) that have long nectar tubes.

Bees can only see four colours clearly: yellow, blue-green, blue and ultra-violet. They perceive red as black. However, this does not mean that bees do not visit red flowers, as any casual observation of a poppy will quickly demonstrate. This is because many flowers have lines or patterns of ultra-violet colour that act as nectar guides to the bees, clearly indicating the way to the source of nectar. The use of native plants is often recommended for wildlife gardens, but bees and butterflies are adaptable creatures and will happily visit exotic plant introductions as long as they can reach the nectar and pollen.

ATTRACTING BEES, BUTTERFLIES & MOTHS

Most butterflies and moths have a long tongue or proboscis and tend to visit plants with many small tubular flowers combined in a large head.

PLANTS TO ATTRACT BUTTERFLIES
- Butterfly bush (*Buddleja davidii*)
- Rowan (*Sorbus aucuparia*)
- *Sedum spectabile*
- Red valerian (*Centranthus ruber*)
- *Verbena bonariensis*
- *Zinnia elegans*
- Poppy (*Papaver*)
- Honeysuckle (*Lonicera periclymenum*)

PLANTS TO ATTRACT MOTHS
- Evening primrose (*Oenothera biennis*)
- Honeysuckle (*Lonicera*)
- Moonflower (*Ipomoea alba*)
- Night-scented stocks (*Matthiola longipetala*)
- Tobacco plant (*Nicotiana sylvestris*)
- White jasmine (*Jasminum officinale*)

PLANTS TO ATTRACT BEES
- Blackberry (*Rubus fruticosus*)
- Lavender (*Lavandula stoechas*)
- Laurustinus (*Viburnum tinus*)
- Bee balm (*Monarda didyma*)
- Catmint (*Nepeta racemosa*)
- Giant yellow hyssop (*Agastache nepetoides*)

Painted Lady on ice plant (Sedum spectabile)

Pyramid moth on thyme (Thymus vulgaris)

Bee on geranium (Pelargonium graveolens)

ABOVE LEFT: *The butterfly bush (*Buddleja davidii*) lives up to its name, in this case attracting peacock butterflies (*Inachis io*).*

LEFT: *The giant knapweed (*Centaurea macrocephala*) has yellow thistle-like heads that are enormously attractive to bees.*

mammals
Because they can cause damage to garden plants, mammals are not always welcome. However, an authentic cottage garden should be animated by all types of wildlife and many mammals have practical benefits. Bats eat insects such as mosquitoes; hedgehogs, shrews and polecats will eat slugs and snails and various insect pests.

TOP: *The European Hedgehog* (Erinaceus europaeus) *is nocturnal and will roll itself into a ball when alarmed.*

ABOVE: *Stack piles of brushwood or position a hedgehog box in a quiet corner to encourage hedgehogs to stay.*

ABOVE RIGHT: *Bat boxes provide artificial roost sites for bats and are important for their conservation.*

Mice and voles

With the exception of dormice, which seem to be universally loved, most small mammals such as mice and voles have long been considered garden pests. Many cottagers kept a cat to control these rodent populations. Mice are not without their uses because they consume snails and insect pests, but you may occasionally have to sacrifice your prized flowers and crops. There are many different species, yellow-necked mice and harvest mice in particular having great charm.

Bats

It is very rewarding in summer to watch these fascinating creatures emerge at dusk. A tiny common pipistrelle (*Pipistrellus pipistrellus*) can eat 3,000 midges and small insects in a night, so they are well worth encouraging as visitors. A small pond or bog garden will give bats somewhere to drink and they will feed on the insects found near water. If you are interested in bats, it is worth contacting your local wildlife trust for information on bat events. In parts of the world where fruit-eating bats are common, however, they are less popular than their insect-eating cousins as a visiting colony can soon strip a tree of fruit and leave deposits of droppings.

If you do not have many trees or shrubs to provide roosting sites, then consider putting up a bat box as high as possible on a sunny wall. Although it may take several years before bats start using a new box, they are a useful way to encourage bats in areas with few natural roosting sites. Commercially made boxes are usually wedge-shaped with a narrow entrance slit at the bottom and a grooved ladder to help the bat access the box. The wood should be rough-sawn so that the bats can grip better and should not be treated with preservatives.

Install bat boxes so they are fixed at least 5m (16ft) above ground level, preferably close to a hedge or tree line, but positioned so that the bats' approach to the box is clear of obstacles. Do not try to open the box to inspect the bats because a special licence is required to disturb or handle bats in many countries.

Hedgehogs

These mammals are useful garden predators that eat almost half their body weight in slugs, snails and caterpillars in a day. They need a safe place to hibernate undisturbed during winter. Hedgehogs often choose a quiet place among piles of leaf litter, under bushy shrubs or in among the leaves of plants such as pampas grass and *Iris unguicularis*, so take care if you are working among these in winter. They also like to use piles of brushwood that may have been stacked for a bonfire, so don't build your bonfire until the day you light it.

Larger mammals

Carnivorous mammals such as stoats, weasels and polecats are common in some areas, but are less often seen because they are shy and nocturnal. They can be useful predators of smaller pest species, but face competition from domestic cats and introduced mink in some regions. Larger animals, such as foxes and badgers, and raccoons in the US, may visit gardens and some species are common in urban areas. Encouraging these will depend on the size of your garden and whether you keep vulnerable livestock such as ducks or chickens.

ATTRACTING WILDLIFE

Squirrels are often seen in daylight, but most mammals usually come out at dusk and are less often seen. Here are various ways of encouraging them.

A log pile gives shelter to mammals.

Heliotrope (H. arborescens)

Blackcurrant (Ribes nigra)

WAYS TO ATTRACT MAMMALS

- Rotting logs and piles of twigs or leaves give shelter and protection to small mammals
- Overgrown areas give shy or elusive animals space to rest and a base from which to forage
- Bat and hedgehog boxes encourage creatures to nest and rest in your garden
- Use native species of trees, plants and shrubs to suit the local wildlife

PLANTS TO ATTRACT BATS

- Common honeysuckle (*Lonicera periclymenum*)
- Common jasmine (*Jasminum officinale*)
- Evening primrose (*Oenothera biennis*)
- Heliotrope (*Heliotropium arborescens*)
- Night scented stock (*Matthiola bicornis*)
- Tobacco plant (*Nicotiana affinis*)

PLANTS TO ATTRACT BADGERS

- Blackberry (*Rubus fruticosus*)
- Blackcurrant (*Ribes nigra*)
- Elderberry (*Sambucus nigra*)
- English oak (*Quercus robur*)
- Black mulberry (*Morus nigra*)

TOP LEFT: *Overgrown gardens provide shelter and protection.*

FAR LEFT: *Foxes (*Vulpes vulpes*) are increasingly common garden visitors but they are likely to be unwelcome if you have chickens.*

LEFT: *Polecats (*Mustela putorius*) are solitary hunters and eat mice, rats and large insects.*

protecting your garden
If you want both fruit and bird song in your garden, you may have to employ some ingenuity so as not to compromise either its productivity or the presence of a diversity of wildlife. Here are some controls that you can use to protect your garden without changing the habits of its wild visitors too much.

ABOVE: *Pea plants covered with wire netting to deter pigeons.*

BELOW: *Strawberries growing in a plastic bag with protective netting to avoid bird damage.*

BELOW RIGHT: *A juvenile blackbird (Turdus merula) collecting redcurrants.*

BELOW FAR RIGHT: *Peg bean netting on to canes to make a temporary fruit frame.*

Protecting crops from birds

Wildlife does not differentiate between the natural environment and your much-loved garden, and birds are as happy plundering your strawberries as they are taking berries from a rowan tree (*Sorbus*) planted for their benefit. Very often, netting vulnerable crops such as brassicas (which pigeons adore) and fruit is the only way for the gardener to produce a good harvest. Individual plants can be protected with bamboo or homemade willow cloches until they are large enough to withstand attack or are ready for harvest.

Sacrificial crops of plants, such as early-fruiting redcurrants, may distract birds from your main harvest, but growing fruit in a fruit cage is often the best solution. They can be expensive, but simple frames may be made by using rubber balls with holes for the insertion of bamboo canes to support netting. Fleece- or netting-covered cloches give protection to low-growing crops such as strawberries, but you need to ensure that pollinating insects have access.

Protecting crops from deer and rabbits

Deer are beautiful, graceful animals with soft, pleading eyes, but are less endearing when they destroy a bed of roses or a newly planted orchard. They are particularly adept at removing spiral tree guards from young plants. Rabbits can also be problematic, especially in the vegetable garden or if they get a taste for your herbaceous perennials. They seem to take a gourmet's delight in new plantings and to expensive additions to the garden in particular. Several proprietary rabbit repellents are available, as well as many traditional deterrents such as eucalyptus oil or human-hair clippings scattered around susceptible plants, most of which tend to work for a short time before the animals become accustomed to them. Sturdy wire netting or electric fencing is the best long-term solution, although obviously expensive.

Protect young trees by driving wooden stakes around the trunk and attaching wire or plastic mesh. Fencing must be at least 60cm (24in) high to deter rabbits and 1.5m (5ft) for deer.

PLANTS RESISTANT TO DEER AND RABBITS

- Bells of Ireland (*Moluccella laevis*)
- Spurge (*Euphorbia*)
- Hellebore (*Helleborus*)
- Hollyhock (*Alcea rosea*)
- Lamb's ears (*Stachys byzantina*)
- Lilac (*Syringa vulgaris*)
- Marvel of Peru (*Mirabilis jalapa*)
- Meadow saffron (*Colchicum autumnale*)
- Mexican orange blossom (*Choisya ternata*)
- Peony (*Paeonia*)
- Snowdrop (*Galanthus nivalis*)
- Spotted laurel (*Aucuba japonica*)
- Strawberry tree (*Arbutus unedo*)
- Yew (*Taxus baccata*)
- Daffodils (*Narcissus*)

Lilac hedge (Syringa vulgaris)

Lamb's ears (Stachys byzantina)

ABOVE: *Fine netting is useful for protecting crops from smaller, often flying pests, such as cabbage whites.*

LEFT: *Temporary netting supported by rubber hoops is a good way of protecting any vulnerable crops (here brassicas) from pests and diseases.*

LEFT: *A mole leaving its tunnel – moles are hard to deter, but if the tunnels expose plant roots you can prevent them from drying out by firming the soil back with the heel of your boot.*

Deer- and rabbit-resistant plants

No plant is totally herbivore-proof. Rabbits and deer will try virtually anything, so the list of less attractive plants above is likely to be greeted by hollow laughter by gardeners. However, generally speaking, in areas with healthy populations of deer and rabbits, planting hairy or aromatic plants, or those with milky sap or tough, leathery leaves, can be effective. Peony (*Paeonia*) leaves, in particular, contain high levels of phenols and are rarely eaten because they taste revolting.

Dealing with moles

While it is unusual to see a mole in the garden, signs of their presence are unmistakable, and the regular tunnelling and upturned heaps of soil can be exasperating. Various repellents, such as sonic devices or pushing mothballs down into the tunnels, are advocated to encourage the moles to move into neighbouring gardens, but are rarely effective for long. The usual alternative of all-out warfare only creates an opening for other moles to move in. Perhaps the most pragmatic response is to accept their presence, replant any plants undermined by tunnelling and to develop an appreciation for regular supplies of beautifully worked potting compost around the garden.

cottage garden plants

When gardening you often find that the plants will choose you rather than the other way around, with your selection dictated by what friends and neighbours have given you, the emergence of spontaneous seedlings and most of all what plants grow best in your conditions. However, choosing more plants to grow in your cottage garden can be one of the most enjoyable aspects. Visiting other gardens or just peering over fences may give you some inspiration. This directory gives a range of suggestions for typical cottage garden plants, grouped into categories to help you select the most appropriate plants for your garden. Plants given the Award of Garden Merit for all-round good performance by the Royal Horticultural Society are indicated by the letters AGM. The hints on cultivation should assist you in growing them successfully. For a key to the hardiness codes, see page 160.

LEFT: Hydrangea aspera *Villosa Group has mauve flowers in late summer.* ABOVE LEFT: *Pear blossom (Pyrus communis) sparkles in the springtime sunlight.* ABOVE CENTRE: *Peony shoots (here Paeonia mascula) are usually a dramatic bronze-red.* ABOVE RIGHT: *Ranunculus ficaria 'Brazen Hussy' is a bronze-leaved celandine with cup-shaped yellow flowers.*

trees
Invaluable for providing height and structure in a garden, trees also add colour, interest, romance and charm through the seasons in your cottage garden. Many trees are available that will be suitable for growing even in the smallest gardens, and if you have more space a wider variety can be included.

ABOVE: *Cercis siliquastrum is a useful tree to give height at the back of a border.*

Arbutus unedo (AGM)
Strawberry tree
Origins: E. Mediterranean and W. Europe, including Ireland
This is a small, evergreen tree, which is often multi-stemmed, with attractive, shredding, red-brown bark. The small, bell-shaped, white flowers develop into red fruits the following year. The fruits are edible, but not particularly appetizing. Arbutus wood is a useful fuel, as it burns very hot.
Height and spread 10m (33ft)
Cultivation Grow in soil rich in organic matter in a sheltered, sunny spot protected from cold winds. It is unusual among members of the Ericaceae family in that it will grow well in limy soils. Propagate from seed sown when ripe or take semi-ripe cuttings in late summer.
Hardiness Fully hardy/Z8
Related plants 'Elfin King' is a compact, free-flowering selection, while A. f. *rubra* has pretty, reddish-pink flowers. *A. menziesii*, the Pacific Madrone or bearberry, from W. North America forms a larger, spreading tree flowering in early summer. It requires acid soil.

Cercis siliquastrum (AGM)
Judas tree
Origins: E. Mediterranean
Fascinating, small tree, with magenta-pink flowers in spring, emerging directly from the bark. As the common name suggests, it is said to be the tree from which Judas Iscariot hanged himself after betraying Christ. The flowers have a mild pea flavour and may be eaten in salads or fried as fritters. *C. s. f. albida* is the white-flowered form of the Judas tree. *C. s.* 'Bodnant' has deep purplish-pink flowers.
Height and spread 10m (33ft)
Cultivation Grows best in a moist, loamy soil in full sun or dappled shade. It is fully hardy once mature, but young plants may require some protection from severe cold. Propagate from seed sown in autumn or take semi-ripe cuttings in summer.
Hardiness Fully hardy/Z6
Related plants *C. canadensis* 'Forest Pansy' is a selection of the Eastern redbud from North America, with deep purple leaves that turn to shades of bronze and red in autumn. *C. chinensis* 'Avondale' is one of the most floriferous plants in the genus. Raised in New Zealand, it has showy, purplish-pink flowers.

Crataegus monogyna
Common hawthorn, May, Quickthorn
Origins: Europe
A thorny, deciduous tree, forming an attractive, domed shape, the hawthorn is more widely used as a hedging plant. The profusion of white blossom was valued for May garlands, and, in Ireland, hawthorn was believed to protect the home from evil on May Day. The wood is used for making walking sticks and tool handles, while the haws are a useful source of food for birds in winter.
Height 10m (33ft); **spread** 8m (26ft)
Cultivation A tolerant tree that will grow on a wide range of soils and is resistant to exposure and pollution. It makes a good, dense hedge, forming a stock-proof barrier when properly laid and maintained. Plants can be grown from seed sown in autumn and left exposed to the winter weather.
Hardiness Fully hardy/Z5

ABOVE: **Arbutus unedo**

ABOVE: **Crataegus monogyna**

Related plants *C. laevigata* 'Paul's Scarlet' (AGM) is an ornamental thorn with double, red flowers. *C. l.* 'Rosea Flore Pleno' has double, dusky-pink flowers. *C. monogyna* 'Biflora', the Glastonbury thorn, is said to have sprung from the staff of St Joseph of Arimathea. It produces flowers and young leaves in mild winters, as well as in spring.

Ilex aquifolium (AGM)
Holly
Origins: W. and S. Europe, W. Asia

Indispensable foliage plants for decorating at Christmas, hollies can be grown as specimen trees, shrubs or hedging. In order to get berries, you need to have a female plant and ensure that there are male plants in the neighbourhood. Do not rely on the cultivar name to indicate a plant's sex: 'Golden Queen' is a male

plant and 'Silver King' is female. There are a number of variegated cultivars such as the female 'Argentea Marginata', which makes a lovely, columnar tree. The heavy, white wood was traditionally used for making chess pieces.
Height 20m (70ft); **spread** 6m (20ft)
Cultivation Grows in most moderately fertile soils and tolerates shade. Variegated varieties produce the best leaf colour in full sun. Trim hedge and topiary specimens from early spring to summer. Hollies can be grown from seed, but germination may be slow. Take semi-ripe cuttings in late summer.
Hardiness Fully hardy/Z7
Related plants *I. crenata*, the box-leaved or Japanese holly, is a small tree or shrub, which can have black, white or yellow berries. The cultivar *I. c.* 'Mariesii' is an extremely slow-growing, dwarf plant with rounded leaves and black fruit.

ABOVE: Prunus 'Kanzan'

ABOVE: Ilex aquifolium 'Silver Queen'

Morus nigra (AGM)
Black mulberry
Origins: S. W. Asia

A rounded tree, the black mulberry has been cultivated since ancient times, although its true origin is uncertain. The fruit ripens to dark purple in late summer, and has a lovely rich flavour, making excellent jams and preserves. Mulberries are not usually sold commercially because they are very soft and do not travel well, so they are best grown at home.
Height 12m (40ft); **spread** 15m (50ft)
Cultivation Grow in full sun in moist, well-drained soil with shelter from cold winds. Prune trees if necessary in late autumn or early winter, otherwise they will 'bleed' sap. Mulberries are usually propagated from thick 'truncheons' of two- to four-year-old wood cut in autumn and treated as hardwood cuttings. Fruit is usually gathered by allowing it to drop on to an old sheet.
Hardiness Fully hardy/Z5
Related plants There are about 10 species of *Morus* found in Africa, Asia and the Americas. The other well-known species is *M. alba*, the white mulberry from China, the leaves of which are used to feed silkworms.

Prunus x subhirtella 'Autumnalis' (AGM)
Higan cherry
Origins: Japan

The Higan cherry is thought to be a hybrid between *P. incisa* and *P. pendula*. It is a spreading, deciduous tree with

toothed leaves that turn yellow and orange in autumn. There are several different selections, but most valued is 'Autumnalis', which has clusters of pink-tinged cherry blossom, borne in mild periods from autumn through to spring.
Height and spread 8m (26ft)
Cultivation Grow in a sunny, sheltered spot in any moist, but well-drained, soil. If pruning is necessary, do so in mid-summer to avoid infection with silver leaf disease. Greenwood cuttings may be taken in early summer, but can be tricky to root.
Hardiness Fully hardy/Z3
Related plants The wild cherry (*P. avium*) has delicate, white blossom in early spring and is also valued for its wood. It was the parent of many ornamental cherries. *P.* 'Kanzan' is a widely planted flowering cherry with profuse clusters of double, candyfloss-pink flowers. *P.* 'Ukon' has elegant, double flowers that open greenish-white, but develop a pink tinge as they age.

Other recommended trees
- *Acer palmatum* (Japanese maple) (AGM)
- *Acacia dealbata* (mimosa) (AGM)
- *Amelanchier asiatica* (snowy mespilus)
- *Asimina triloba* (hardy pawpaw)
- *Chimonanthus virginicus* (fringe tree)
- *Euonymus europaeus* (spindle tree) (AGM)
- *Malus x zumi* 'Golden Hornet' (crab apple) (AGM)
- *Mespilus germanica* (medlar)
- *Sorbus aucuparia* (rowan) (AGM)
- *Taxus baccata* (common yew) (AGM)

ABOVE: Prunus x subhirtella 'Autumnalis' is the longest-flowering cherry.

shrubs

Mix evergreen and deciduous shrubs to give an interesting backbone to the garden. If little space is available, choose cottage-garden-style shrubs that provide more than one season of interest, such as viburnums with pretty flowers in spring followed by berries to attract wildlife in autumn and winter.

ABOVE: **Daphne cneorum 'Eximia' has wonderfully fragrant, dainty flowers.**

Daphne mezereum
Daphne, mezereon
Origins: Europe, Caucasus and Turkey

This sweetly scented, deciduous shrub has long been treasured for its winter and early spring flowers. The most commonly seen daphne has purplish-pink flowers followed by poisonous, scarlet berries. There is, however, a white-flowered variant, *D. m.* f. *alba*, which has yellowish berries and is often a more vigorous plant.
Height and spread 1.2m (4ft)

Cultivation Grows best in loamy, well-drained soil in sun or partial shade. Keep pruning to a minimum and try to avoid transplanting specimens. Daphnes are prone to virus and can die unexpectedly, so propagate regularly to have a supply of replacement plants. Seed should be sown as soon as it is ripe. Take softwood cuttings in early summer or layer stems in spring. Ensure that no part of the plant is eaten by children or livestock.
Hardiness Fully hardy/Z4

Related plants *D. cneorum* 'Eximia' is one of the easiest of daphnes to grow. It is a low-growing, evergreen shrub with fragrant, rose-pink flowers opening from darker buds in late spring. *D. x burkwoodii* 'Somerset' is a small, upright shrub with plentiful pink flowers at cherry-blossom time.

Lonicera x purpusii (AGM)
Winter honeysuckle
Origins: China

L. x purpusii is a hybrid between *L. fragrantissima* and *L. standishii*, both in themselves valuable winter-flowering shrubs, but now surpassed by their progeny. The cultivar 'Winter Beauty' bears an abundance of sweetly scented, white flowers throughout winter and spring. Outside of the flowering season it can look fairly ungainly, but it can be used as a climbing frame for lightweight climbers.
Height and spread 1.5m (5ft)
Cultivation Easy to grow in any well-drained soil in sun or dappled shade. Prune after flowering from time to time to rejuvenate the plant. It makes a good informal hedge and plants can be fan-trained against a wall. Propagate from hardwood cuttings in autumn or winter.

ABOVE: **Myrtus communis**

Low shoots frequently layer themselves and the layers can be lifted in winter.
Hardiness Fully hardy/Z6
Related plants *L. elisae* has bronze foliage and larger, fragile-looking, bell-shaped flowers that are only lightly scented. *L. setifera* has erect, bristly stems and daphne-like, pink flowers from late winter.

Myrtus communis (AGM)
Myrtle
Origins: Mediterranean

The myrtle has aromatic leaves and fragrant, white flowers with clusters of stamens like pins in a pincushion. It is a bushy, evergreen shrub that can grow to 3m (10ft) tall, although *M. c.* subsp. *tarentina* is more compact. In many Mediterranean countries, sprigs of myrtle were incorporated into bridal bouquets. The berries are used to flavour liqueurs and as a spice in the Middle East.
Height and spread 3m (10ft)
Cultivation Requires a well-drained soil and does best in a sheltered, sunny site. In mild climates, myrtles can make an ornamental hedge. Propagate from summer cuttings or those sprigs in the bridal bouquet. Seeds can be sown in autumn or spring.
Hardiness Frost hardy/Z8
Related plants The double-flowered Mediterranean myrtle, *M. communis* 'Flore Pleno', is quite rare. Variegated leaf forms are more widely available and provide useful foliage for flower arrangers. *Luma apiculata* is a beautiful species from Chile, often seen as a multi-stemmed tree with peeling bark. It has white flowers in late summer and autumn and, after hot summers, produces edible, red and black fruits.

Paeonia suffruticosa
Tree peony
Origins: China

Tree peonies have flamboyant flowers with silky petals in vibrant colours. They have an ancient history in China where they are known as 'mudan'. Many plants imported from Japan in Edwardian times were renamed to honour famous people. 'Cardinal Vaughan' has semi-double flowers in a rich ruby-purple. 'Duchess of Marlborough' is a delicate pink.

Height and spread 2.2m (7ft)

Cultivation Grow in sun or dappled shade in any reasonably fertile soil. Leggy plants can be pruned back. Watch out for suckers from the herbaceous rootstock on grafted plants. Tree peonies are easy to propagate from seed, but they can take many years to flower.

Hardiness Fully hardy/Z5

Related plants *P. ludlowii* is a vigorous species from Tibet with golden yellow flowers and handsome foliage. *P. x lemoinei* 'High Noon' has semi-double, lemon flowers with reddish flares at the centre of the petals. *P. rockii*, with white flowers blotched maroon in the centre, is something of a cult plant, sold at prices that reflect its desirability. Raising plants from seed is the more affordable option.

Rosa canina
Dog rose
Origins: Asia, Europe and N. Africa

Roses in some shape or form are essential in the cottage garden, but there is a huge range and choosing which rose to start with can be daunting. The wild dog rose (*R. canina*) is a vigorous shrub, with masses of single, fragrant flowers that give way to juicy, red hips. It is perhaps too energetic for most gardens, but is lovely when allowed to romp through an informal hedge.

Height up to 5m (16ft); **spread** indefinite

Cultivation Roses are fairly tolerant plants, but generally prefer an open site in full sun. They like a humus-rich, fertile, moist but well-drained soil. Propagate cultivars by hardwood cuttings taken in autumn, which ensures that plants will not sucker from the rootstock.

Hardiness Fully hardy/Z3

Related plants The sweet briar or eglantine (*R. rubiginosa*), known for its apple-scented foliage, has inspired artists and poets for many centuries. Good rose cultivars include *R. gallica* 'Versicolor', widely known as 'Rosa Mundi', with pink-and-white-striped flowers. *R.* 'Ballerina', introduced in 1937, is a polyantha rose which puts on a show of small, apple-blossom pink flowers from summer through to autumn. *R.* 'Dusky Maiden' (1947) is a single rose with wavy-edged petals of pure red velvet. *R.* 'Helen Knight' (1966), a hybrid of *R. ecae*, is one of several similar, early-flowering, single, clear yellow roses that combine well with blue ceanothus.

Syringa vulgaris (AGM)
Lilac
Origins: E. Europe

Lilac is a much-loved, fragrant shrub traditionally planted by the cottage

ABOVE: Paeonia suffruticosa *has jagged leaves and spectacular flowers.*

door so that its scent could be enjoyed. Lilacs are sometimes criticized for their lack of attraction after flowering, but the deep green, heart-shaped leaves make a good backdrop to summer performers. Old plants can get gnarled and tree-like, and make excellent supports for late-flowering clematis. There is a huge range of garden lilacs to choose from: 'Decaisne' has single, purplish flowers; 'Primrose' opens yellowish-cream, fading to a creamy white; and 'Madame Lemoine' has large, double, white flowers.

Height and spread 5m (16ft)

Cultivation Grow in fertile, neutral to chalky soils in full sun or dappled shade. Prune if necessary immediately after flowering. Over-large plants will tolerate hard pruning to rejuvenate them. Propagate by greenwood cuttings in early summer; excluding light from the stem with black plastic for some weeks before taking the cutting will increase the success rate.

Hardiness Fully hardy/Z5

Related plants *S. x hyacinthiflora* 'Esther Staley' is a large shrub with a profusion of pink flowers opening from reddish buds. *S. meyeri* 'Palibin' is a slow-growing lilac for the tiniest of gardens. It has small, neat leaves and fragrant, lilac-pink flowers.

Other recommended shrubs

- *Buddleja davidii* (butterfly bush) (AGM)
- *Chaenomeles speciosa* (flowering quince) (AGM)
- *Choisya ternata* (Mexican orange blossom) (AGM)
- *Elaeagnus angustifolia* (oleaster) (AGM)
- *Philadelphus coronarius* (mock orange) (AGM)

ABOVE: **Syringa vulgaris**

ABOVE: **Rosa canina**

climbers

Climbing plants add extra interest to trees and shrubs, and are attractive features in their own right, scrambling over walls and trellises and helping to evoke the informal abundance of a cottage garden. Be careful, however, to select climbers that will not be too vigorous for the intended site.

Clematis viticella (AGM)
Clematis, Virgin's bower
Origins: S. Europe

The late-summer-flowering *C. viticella* was one of the first clematis to be grown in gardens and is still popular for its ease of growth and prolific flowers. 'Flore Pleno' (syn. 'Mary Rose') has dusky purple, double flowers in great profusion. There are a number of different hybrids of *C. viticella*, such as *C.* 'Madame Julia Correvon' with velvety, wine-red flowers; the pale lilac, fragrant *C.* 'Betty Corning'; and the double-flowered *C.* 'Purpurea Plena Elegans'. They are all excellent plants for covering a trellis or scrambling through shrubs.
Height 2–3m (6½–10ft)
Cultivation Grow in a fertile soil, rich in organic matter, in full sun or dappled shade. Clematis usually benefit from their root area being shaded to prevent drying out. *Viticella*-type clematis are pruned by cutting all the stems back to about 15cm (6in) above soil level in late winter.
Hardiness Fully hardy/Z5
Related plants *C. alpina* is a spring-flowering plant with nodding flowers that are usually blue, but various hybrids are grown such as *C.* 'White Columbine', and *C.* 'Ruby', with rose-red flowers. The vigorous *C. armandii* is an evergreen climber with long, leathery leaves. It produces a cloud of creamy, scented flowers in mid-spring.

Ipomoea tricolor (AGM)
Morning glory
Origins: Tropical C. and S. America

This twining annual is a beautiful plant with which to cover a trellis, or it can be used to add summer interest to a spring-flowering shrub. The trumpet-shaped, usually sky-blue or purple flowers open in the morning, appearing in a long succession throughout summer. The most widely grown variety is 'Heavenly Blue', which has rich azure flowers with a white eye. The seed strain 'Flying Saucers' has flowers that are striped blue and white.
Height to 3m (10ft)
Cultivation Soak seed overnight before sowing singly in pots in spring. Plant out after all danger of frosts has passed. Grow in a moderately fertile soil in full sun with shelter from cold winds. Cuttings will root quickly in a glass of water on the windowsill.

ABOVE: **Lonicera x italica** *is a particularly colourful and fragrant honeysuckle.*

Hardiness Frost tender/Z9
Related plants The moonflower (*I. alba*) is very fast-growing and has scented, white flowers that open in the evening. *I. quamoclit*, with feathery leaves and a profusion of vivid scarlet flowers, originates from tropical South America. There is a white form called 'White Feather'. The Spanish flag (*I. lobata*, syn. *I. versicolor*) has narrow, tubular flowers that open red, fading through orange and yellow to white.

Jasminum officinale (AGM)
Jasmine, jessamine
Origins: Asia Minor, Himalayas and China

The common jasmine is a vigorous climber, with small, heavily scented, white flowers from summer through to autumn. The cultivar 'Clotted Cream' has creamy white flowers. 'Argenteovariegatum' has leaves variegated in creamy white. There is a golden-leaved form called 'Fiona Sunrise'.
Height to 12m (40ft)

ABOVE: **Clematis viticella** *'Flore Pleno'*

ABOVE: **Ipomoea tricolor** *'Heavenly Blue'*

ABOVE: Lathyrus odoratus

Cultivation Grow in well-drained soil in sun or dappled shade. Thin old and overcrowded shoots after flowering. Propagate from semi-ripe cuttings in summer or layer in autumn.
Hardiness Frost hardy/Z7
Related plants The winter-flowering jasmine (*J. nudiflorum*) from China is an arching shrub that will scramble through a hedge or can be trained up a wall. It is valued for its primrose-yellow, but sadly unscented, flowers in winter and early spring. *J. beesianum* is evergreen in mild climates. It produces lightly fragrant, deep pink flowers in summer. The Arabic jasmine (*J. sambac*) is the national flower of Indonesia. Like the Chinese *J. paniculatum*, it is used to make jasmine tea. Both these species would need to be grown in a glasshouse in temperate climates.

Lathyrus odoratus (AGM)
Sweet pea
Origins: Italy
One of the best-loved of cottage-garden annuals, the sweet pea is grown for its colourful, often sweetly-scented, flowers. The cultivar 'Cupani', introduced by Father Francis Cupani to England in 1695, is still available; it has small flowers with a maroon standard and mauve wings, as well as an intense fragrance. Most selections climb to around 2m (6½ft) by means of tendrils, although there are also non-climbing, bush forms.
Height to 3m (10ft)

Cultivation Soak seed, then sow in containers in a cold frame in early spring or outdoors in mid-spring. Earlier flowers can be obtained by sowing in autumn. Grow in fertile soil in an open, sunny site. Pick flowers regularly to ensure a summer-long display.
Hardiness Fully hardy/Z4
Related plants The everlasting pea (*L. latifolius*) is a vigorous perennial climber with profuse, pink to purple, unscented flowers. There is a pure white form called 'White Pearl'. *L. nervosus*, Lord Anson's pea from South America, is a herbaceous perennial climber with grey-green leaves and fragrant, purplish-blue flowers. *L. sativus*, has small, pure blue flowers.

Lonicera x italica (AGM)
Honeysuckle
Origins: Europe
A vigorous, deciduous climber, this is a hybrid between *L. caprifolium* and *L. etrusca*. It is a richly coloured and very free-flowering honeysuckle, festooned with fragrant flowers from late spring until mid-summer. *L. x americana* is an evergreen plant with softer coloured, pink and cream flowers from mid-summer until the autumn.
Height to 7m (23ft)
Cultivation Plant in any fertile soil in full sun or partial shade. To control growth, prune after flowering. Overlarge plants will tolerate hard pruning. Propagate by semi-ripe cuttings in summer, or, if you do not mind variable offspring, from seed sown as the berries ripen.
Hardiness Fully hardy/Z4
Related plants *L. periclymenum* is the common honeysuckle or woodbine, with very fragrant flowers. The cultivar 'Graham Thomas' has a particularly long flowering season. The Mediterranean *L. etrusca* 'Superba' is a vigorous honeysuckle for a sunny site, with cream and yellow flowers in high summer. The Chinese species *L. tragophylla* has bronze-tinted, young leaves and pure yellow flowers. It is best grown in shade.

Rosa banksiae (AGM)
Banksia rose
Origins: W. and C. China
This is a vigorous climber with long, slender stems. The wild plant is single-flowered, but there are also yellow and

white, double forms. The yellow form 'Lutea' is probably the most popular, but both double-flowered plants give a stunning display in late spring, especially combined with lilac-coloured wisteria.
Height 10m (33ft)
Cultivation Less hardy than many other roses, the banksia rose benefits from a sheltered spot or sunny wall. Grow in any free-draining soil. In cold areas, mulch in late autumn to protect the roots from penetrating frosts. Pruning is only required if it outgrows its allotted area. The banksia rose is virtually thornless, which is a definite advantage when training against a wall.
Hardiness Fully hardy/Z7

Related plants *R.* 'Climbing Étoile de Hollande' is a much-loved rose with very fragrant, double, deep crimson flowers. *R.* 'American Pillar' is a rampant rambler with profuse clusters of white-eyed, carmine-pink flowers in mid-summer. *R.* 'Violette', introduced in 1921, is a lightly thorned rambler with unusual, mauve-coloured, semi-double flowers. *R.* 'Paul's Himalayan Musk' is a rampant climber, covering itself in masses of double, soft pink, richly fragrant flowers.

Other recommended climbers
- *Humulus lupulus* (hop) (AGM)
- *Passiflora caerulea* (blue passion flower) (AGM)
- *Thunbergia alata* (black-eyed Susan)

ABOVE: Rosa banksiae *'Lutea' has delightful lemon, button-like flowers.*

perennials
Combine classic cottage garden favourites such as peonies, campanulas and columbines with interesting new selections of heucheras and hostas to give a display that is fresh and lively year after year. Most perennials are easily propagated so that you can swap plants with friends.

ABOVE: **Aquilegia vulgaris** *comes in a wide range of colours and forms.*

Aquilegia vulgaris
Columbine
Origins: Europe
These plants have ferny foliage and pretty flowers that usually have long, nectar-rich spurs, loved by bumble bees. Plants in the *stellata* group have flat, starry, spurless flowers in various colours, including green. 'Nora Barlow' has neatly double flowers in dusky pink, tinted with green and white. *A. v.* 'William Guiness' is single with deep plum-black sepals and a white skirt.

Height 1m (3ft); spread 50cm (20in)
Cultivation Columbines are tolerant plants that will grow in sun or light shade in any soil that is not too dry. They self-seed generously, but are promiscuous, and so the cultivars are unlikely to come true from seed.
Hardiness Fully hardy/Z4
Related plants *A. fragrans* is softly coloured with a sweet fragrance. The dainty *A. alpina* usually has blue flowers and long, straight spurs. The North American *A. formosa* has small,

red and yellow flowers, which are pollinated by hummingbirds in their native land.

Aster novi-belgii (AGM)
Michaelmas daisy, New York aster, Starwort
Origins: N. America
The term Michaelmas daisy is popularly applied to those asters and their cultivars that are in flower on the feast day of St Michael, which, in Britain, was celebrated on 29 September. They are useful, late-flowering plants to bring colour to the garden when the main summer flush of flowers is over. They provide a rich supply of nectar for butterflies. 'Alice Haslam' is one of the first to flower. It is a short plant, with deep red-pink flowers. Pale pink 'Fellowship' is a medium-height variety with double flowers. Mauve-pink 'Autumn Rose' is very late-flowering.
Height 90cm (36in); spread 20–75cm (8–30in)
Cultivation Michaelmas daisies prefer a fertile, moist soil in sun or light shade. They can be prone to powdery mildew in dry seasons. Divide every three years in spring or autumn.

Hardiness Fully hardy/Z2
Related plants The New England aster (*A. novae-anglia*) is a robust, long-lived plant, more resistant to mildew. The rose-pink cultivar 'Harrington's Pink' was found growing wild in Quebec, and introduced to England in 1943. *A. divaricatus* is a late, white-flowering species, useful in that it will thrive in a shaded spot under trees.

Campanula persicifolia (AGM)
Bellflower, Peach-leaved bellflower
Origins: S. Europe, W. and N. Asia
A classic border plant with slender stems, bearing cup-shaped flowers in white or shades of blue-lilac. There are a number of double-flowered cultivars, including the charmingly named 'Blue Bloomers' and white 'Alba Coronata'. Plants spread slowly by means of slender rhizomes.
Height 1m (3ft); spread 30cm (1ft)
Cultivation Grows best in a fertile, neutral to alkaline soil in full sun or dappled shade. Related species such as the nettle-leaved bellflower (*C. trachelium*) and *C. pyramidalis* will thrive even in dry soils. Propagate by division in autumn or spring, or from seed sown in spring. Plants will self-seed

ABOVE: **Campanula persicifolia**

ABOVE: **Cardamine pratensis**

generously, so cut back after flowering to keep special cultivars true.
Hardiness Fully hardy/Z3
Related plants The giant bellflower (*C. latifolia*) is a striking plant for a shady woodland border. *C. rapunculus* is a European species once cultivated for its edible tubers, which are called rampions. The biennial Canterbury bell (*C. medium*) is a classic cottage-garden plant, particularly in the cup-and-saucer form 'Calycanthema', in which there is a saucer-like rim at the base of the cup-like flower.

Cardamine pratensis
Lady's smock, Cuckoo flower, Milkmaids, Toothwort
Origins: Europe, including the British Isles

A common wild flower of damp meadows and riverbanks, in many parts of Britain the first flowering of the cuckoo flower coincides with the springtime arrival of the cuckoo from Africa. It is a delicate plant, with sprays of pale pink, soft lilac or white flowers. Double-flowered cultivars such as 'Flore Pleno' and 'William' are less appealing to bees, but of equal value as a food plant for the caterpillars of orange-tipped and various other butterflies.
Height 45cm (18in); **spread** 30cm (12in)
Cultivation Grow in any moist soil in full sun or partial shade. Propagate by division in spring or autumn, or by seed sown as soon as it is ripe. *C. pratensis*

ABOVE: **Dianthus 'Mrs Sinkins'**

sometimes produces plantlets on its leaves which can be removed and potted on.
Hardiness Fully hardy/Z4
Related plants Formerly in the separate genus, *Dentaria*, the toothworts have unusual underground rhizomes like strings of teeth. They make excellent woodland plants. *C. enneaphylla* has dark, bronze-tinged leaves and nodding, creamy yellow flowers. *C. pentaphylla* forms a compact clump with lilac-pink flowers. *C. quinquefolia*, with soft purple flowers, can be rampant, but is valuable for its early flowering at snowdrop time. It dies down quickly after flowering, and so can be allowed to romp among later-flowering perennials.

Delphinium elatum (AGM)
Delphinium
Origins: Pyrenees to Siberia

The most common garden delphiniums are cultivars of the Elatum Group. At their best these are wonderful plants, with tall spires of velvety flowers in shades of pure blue, purple, pink or white. Plants bought from garden centres vary so go to a specialist. Look out for *D.* 'Blue Nile', mid-blue with a white eye; *D.* 'Pericles', sky blue; *D.* 'Fenella', rich blue with a dark eye; *D.* 'Olive Poppleton', white with a brown eye; *D.* 'Sunkissed', cream; and *D.* 'Summerfield Miranda', soft pink.
Height 1.5–2m (5–6½ft); **spread** 60–90cm (2–3ft)
Cultivation Grow in a fertile, well-drained soil in full sun. Taller cultivars will need staking. Water in dry weather. Plants will benefit from a liquid feed every two weeks in the growing season. Propagate from basal cuttings in early spring or seed sown at the same time.
Hardiness Fully hardy/Z3
Related plants The Belladonna hybrids, such as 'Atlantis' (gentian blue), 'Casa Blanca' (white) and 'Cliveden Beauty' (light blue), are reliable perennials with light, wiry stems. *D. semibarbatum* is an unusual, yellow-flowered species from Afghanistan. It is usually short-lived, but can self-seed. *D. cardinale* from California has vivid red, long-spurred flowers. *D. nudicaule* is another of the red-flowered American species.

ABOVE: Delphinium *Belladonna Group 'Atlantis' is a long-lived cultivar.*

Dianthus plumarius
Pinks, Gillyflower
Origins: E. Europe

The old-fashioned pinks of the 19th century are mainly derived from this highly fragrant species. The petals are deeply fringed or 'pinked'. Among the best known is the shaggy, white-flowered *D.* 'Mrs Sinkins'. In Chaucer's time, pinks were called sops-in-wine, referring to their use in flavouring drinks. The plant grown as the cultivar 'Sops-in-wine' today has double, white flowers with a crimson heart.
Height and spread 30cm (1ft)
Cultivation Grows in any well-drained soil and flourishes on chalk. It flowers best in full sun. Propagate from cuttings.
Hardiness Fully hardy/Z3
Related plants The Cheddar pink (*D. gratianopolitanus*, syn. *D. caesius*) is usually short-lived, but is worth sowing seed every year or so to enjoy its rich fragrance. Malmaison carnations were popular in the late 19th century for their flowers' intense clove fragrance. Only a few cultivars survive: *D.* 'Souvenir de la Malmaison' is a blush pink and *D.* 'Tayside Red' a deep red.

Geranium x magnificum (AGM)
Cranesbill, Hardy geranium
Origins: Of garden origin

Geraniums are reliable, easy-to-grow plants. *G. x magnificum* is a vigorous plant with softly hairy leaves and a profusion of rich violet flowers in mid-summer. It is beautiful as ground cover under roses. 'Rosemoor' is a more compact plant, less inclined to flop.
Height 45cm (18in); **spread** 60cm (2ft)
Cultivation Tolerates most soils, unless waterlogged, in sun or dappled shade. Shear plants down after flowering for a fresh leaf crop. Propagate by division.
Hardiness Fully hardy/Z4
Related plants One of the best geraniums for ground cover is the semi-evergreen *G. macrorrhizum*, with strongly aromatic leaves. It flowers well even in shade. The usual form has magenta flowers, but look out for 'Snow Sprite', a neat, white-flowered variety. *G. wlassovianum* has long-lasting, pinkish purple flowers and leaves that turn to shades of orange and red in autumn. *G.* 'Patricia' is a hybrid geranium with vivid pink-magenta flowers over a long period. It grows well even in dry chalk soils.

ABOVE: *Iris pallida 'Variegata'* has leaves and stems strongly striped with cream.

are excellent for a mixed border. The Spuria irises, a beardless type, including *I. orientalis* and cultivars such as *I.* 'Sunset Colors', are tall, robust plants. They are easy to grow in sun or partial shade and will even compete with rough grasses in an orchard-type setting.

Paeonia officinalis (AGM)
Peony
Origins: Europe

Grown in monastery gardens as a medicinal and an ornamental plant since the Middle Ages, *P. officinalis* was known as the female peony because its leaves are finer than those of the 'male' peony, *P. mascula*. The best-known is the robust cottage peony *P. officinalis* 'Rubra Plena'. The double, deep reddish flowers require support. 'Rosea Superba Plena' has ruffled, rose-pink flowers. The single form 'China Rose' has silky, pink petals.

Height and spread 60cm (2ft)
Cultivation Flourishes in fertile, well-drained soil in sun or partial shade. They are long-lived plants, not usually eaten by deer, rabbits, slugs or aphids. The fungal disease peony blight may be a problem in wet seasons. Peonies are easy, albeit slow, from seed or can be divided in autumn.
Hardiness Fully hardy/Z4
Related plants Affectionately known as Molly the Witch, *P. mlokosewitschii* has single, lemon-yellow flowers of great beauty. *P.* 'Late Windflower', a hybrid of the Himalayan peony *P. emodi*, is a tall plant with nodding, white flowers.

Crimson *P.* 'Buckeye Belle' is a robust hybrid for sunny sites. Rose-scented *P.* 'White Cap' has a ring of vivid, reddish petals surrounding a mass of creamy white petaloids.

Papaver orientale (AGM)
Oriental poppy
Origins: W. Asia

Most cultivated Oriental poppies are hybrids derived from three Asian species. They are bold plants with jagged, bristly leaves and large, bowl-shaped flowers in early summer. They usually die back after flowering and so are best planted in a mixed border among later-flowering perennials such as asters. 'Beauty of Livermere' is a tall cultivar with deep crimson flowers. 'Karine' is more delicate with salmon-pink petals stained purple at the base. 'Black and White' is the best white cultivar with prominent black blotches at each petal base.

Height 1m (3ft); **spread** 30cm–1m (1–3ft)
Cultivation Oriental poppies will grow in any well-drained soil in a sunny position. The larger cultivars may require staking. They are usually propagated by root cuttings, and any fragments of root left in the ground when a plant is moved may grow to form a new plant.
Hardiness Fully hardy/Z3
Related plants *P. spicatum* is an unusual poppy with stiff stems carrying several soft, terracotta-coloured flowers. A native of southern Turkey, it grows best in a warm, dry soil. *Meconopsis cambrica*, the Welsh poppy, is very easy

Iris (Bearded Group)
Bearded iris
Origins: Of garden origin

Bearded irises have thick, woody rhizomes carrying fans of sword-like foliage. First to bloom are the dwarf bearded irises such as 'Austrian Sky'. Intermediate varieties follow on in late spring, with the tall cultivars extending the season into mid-summer. There is a huge range of colours, petal textures and fragrances to choose from. 'Dusky Challenger' is a dramatic cultivar with silky, deep violet petals and a chocolate scent. 'Silver Shower' has large, lacy, white flowers with a contrasting red beard and rich, fruity fragrance. 'Before the Storm' has

black, velvet flowers. The old cultivar *I. pallida* 'Variegata' has attractively striped leaves.

Height Standard dwarf: 20–40cm (8–16in); Intermediate: 40–70cm (16–28in); Tall: 70cm (28in)
Cultivation Prefers a sunny spot in well-drained, preferably neutral to limy soil. Do not overcrowd, and clear away old leaves and debris to allow the sun to warm the rhizomes. Some tall cultivars may need staking. Divide after flowering every three to four years.
Hardiness Fully hardy/Z4
Related plants Beardless Siberian irises (*I. sibirica*), such as pale blue 'Perry's Blue', white and yellow 'Butter and Sugar' and 'Dirigo Black Velvet',

ABOVE: Iris *'Edward of Windsor'*

ABOVE: Papaver orientale

ABOVE: Paeonia 'Late Windflower' is a robust peony that suits woodland areas.

ABOVE: Pulsatilla vulgaris have jewel-bright flowers and ferny leaves.

to grow and seeds itself around. Seed-raised plants will give a mixture of orange, yellow and reddish flowers. The Himalayan blue poppy (*M. betonicifolia*) and its relatives are difficult to establish, requiring cool, moist summers. In favoured gardens, they may naturalize.

Primula vulgaris (AGM)
Primrose
Origins: Europe and W. Turkey

With its rosettes of evergreen leaves and fragrant, pale lemon-yellow flowers, the primrose is a valued plant. In areas where they grow in great numbers, they used to be sent to markets packed in moss to keep them fresh. Flowers cut when young can last a fortnight in water.

Height 20cm (8in); **spread** 35cm (14in)
Cultivation Prefer damp conditions and a rich, fertile soil. They will grow in shade, but flower best in full light. They can be surprisingly adaptable. Propagate from seed or divide after flowering.
Hardiness Fully hardy/Z5
Related plants Cowslips (*P. veris*) have long stalks of fragrant, orange-marked, yellow flowers. *P. juliae* from the Caucasus has magenta flowers.

Pulsatilla vulgaris (AGM)
Pasque flower
Origins: Europe

A herbaceous perennial of undisturbed chalk grasslands, the Pasque flower blooms around Easter time, which gives it the common name Pasque, meaning "of Easter". It has a clump formation and has attractive, ferny foliage and showy, purple flowers, erect or nodding, opening from buds that are covered in kitten-soft, silvery hairs. The flowers are followed by striking, silky seedheads. Boiling the purple flowers produces a green dye that, in the time of Edward I of England (1239–1307), was used to colour Easter eggs. There is a white form, 'Alba', and a seed strain 'Barton's Pink' with baby-pink flowers. 'Eva Constance' is compact with deep red flowers. Double forms and those with fringed petals are sometimes available.

Height and spread 20–30cm (8–12in)
Cultivation Pulsatillas grow best in a free-draining soil in full sun. They do not take well to being transplanted and can be hard to establish. Propagate from seed sown as soon as it is ripe.
Hardiness Fully hardy/Z5
Related plants There are around 30 species of pulsatilla, many of which are best grown in a raised bed or alpine garden rather than a mixed border. *P. occidentalis* from North America prefers acid soils. *P. pratensis* subsp. *nigricans* has flowers of such a deep purple that they look black. The dainty flowers nod when first open, but as they mature they face the sky. The alpine pulsatilla *P. alpina* has upward-facing white flowers.

bulbs, corms & tubers

Bulbs such as daffodils (*Narcissus*), corms such as crocus and tubers like *Cyclamen hederifolium* all have underground storage organs. They are versatile and can be layered under other plants. If the bulbs naturalize, the colour they bring to your cottage garden will improve year on year.

ABOVE: **Anemone nemorosa**

Anemone nemorosa (AGM)
Wood anemone, Windflower, Grandmother's nightcap
Origins: Europe

A creeping perennial growing from thin, twig-like rhizomes, the wood anemone is a common European native and a good indicator of ancient woodland. Generally white-flowered, wild colonies with purple- or pink-tinted flowers are not unusual. There are many different cultivars, of which 'Robinsoniana', with large, lavender flowers, is one of the best. 'Vestal' is the best double with neat, white flowers. 'Virescens' is a curiosity in which the petals have been replaced by green, leaf-like bracts.
Height 15cm (6in); **spread** 30cm (12in)
Cultivation Plant rhizomes in autumn in moist soil, rich in organic matter, in dappled shade. Full sun is tolerated, as long as the soil remains moist in summer. Propagate by splitting the rhizomes in autumn. Mediterranean species require more sun and a well-drained soil.
Hardiness Fully hardy/Z4
Related plants *A. ranunculoides* is a vigorous plant with deep yellow flowers. *A. blanda* has knobbly tubers which increase quickly to form spreading clumps. The starry flowers are usually violet-blue, but there are white and pink selections. *A. coronaria* from the Mediterranean is the parent of many cultivars in the De Caen Group, including the semi-double white 'The Bride' and the blue 'Lord Lieutenant'.

Colchicum autumnale (AGM)
Meadow saffron, Naked ladies, Autumn crocus, Dainty maidens
Origins: Europe

Colchicums share with nerines the common name of naked ladies because they both flower unclothed by leaves. The autumn flowers of colchicums look like particularly large crocuses, but they can be easily distinguished by counting the stamens: colchicums have six stamens whereas crocuses, being members of the iris family, have three. It is important not to confuse the two because, unlike the true saffron, colchicums are poisonous. They contain the alkaloid colchicines which is used medicinally in the treatment of gouty arthritis, but can be very toxic. The flowers are followed by handsome, glossy leaves. Cut off the leaves when they start to look shabby in late spring.
Height and spread 10–15cm (4–6in)
Cultivation Meadow saffron grows wild in rich, damp meadows or light woodland. Plant the corms in late summer, or they can be flowered dry on the windowsill and planted afterwards. It is the hardiest species of colchicum.
Hardiness Fully hardy/Z4
Related plants *C. speciosum* is a robust species with large, goblet-shaped flowers that are particularly beautiful in the pure white form 'Album'. *C.* 'Waterlily' has lovely, double, pinkish lilac flowers, which, sadly, are easily spoilt by bad weather. *C. agrippium* has smaller flowers which have an attractive checkered pattern to them. The leaves are less inclined to flop than in some of the cultivars.

Crocus tommasinianus (AGM)
Crocus, Tommies
Origins: E. Europe

This slender crocus is one of the first to flower each year. Flower colour varies from silvery lilac to reddish purple and pink-tinged, and there is also a white form. It increases freely by offsets and seed, and will naturalize in grass or even between paving slabs.
Height 10cm (4in); **spread** 2.5–8cm (1–3in)
Cultivation Easy to grow in any soil in sun or partial shade. Most other crocuses flower better in full sun.
Hardiness Fully hardy/Z4

ABOVE: **Crocus tommasinianus** *is one of the first crocuses to bloom and is adored by bees.*

ABOVE: Narcissus pseudonarcissus

L. lancifolium is the well-known tiger lily with spotted orange or yellow flowers. It prefers a moist, acid soil. There is a double form, 'Flore Pleno'.

Narcissus pseudonarcissus (AGM)
Wild daffodil, Daffydowndilly, Lent lily, Gooseflop
Origins: W. Europe, including the British Isles

N. pseudonarcissus is the narcissus to choose for those wanting a Wordsworthian "host of golden daffodils". In the 16th century, it grew in great profusion throughout much of the United Kingdom, but it now has a very disjointed distribution. The typical form has pale yellow petals with a slightly darker trumpet. Occasional double-flowered sports occur in the wild.

Height 15–30cm (6–12in)

Cultivation Plant bulbs at twice their own depth in autumn, preferably in a fertile, well-drained soil that is moist in spring. A sunny position is best to promote flowering. Lift and divide clumps every few years to retain vigour.

Hardiness Fully hardy/Z4

Related plants The Tenby daffodil (N. obvallaris) has small, uniformly yellow flowers. The poet's narcissus (N. poeticus) has pure white petals and a short, red-rimmed trumpet. N. poeticus var. physaloides is unusual in that the buds are inflated. The shaggy double form 'Plenus' is intensely fragrant. The van Sion daffodil, N. 'Telamonius Plenus', is a variable

ABOVE: Lilium candidum

double with greenish-yellow flowers and a long blooming time – it is robust and ideal for naturalizing.

Tigridia pavonia
Tiger flower, Peacock flower, Jockey's cap
Origins: Mexico

Summer-flowering tiger flowers have long, pleated leaves and a succession of short-lived, but flamboyant, flowers. The usual form has vivid red petals, but bulbs are also available with orange, pink, yellow and white flowers, usually with a spotted central cap.

Height 45cm (18in); **spread** 10–15cm (4–6in)

Cultivation Grow in a freely draining soil in full sun. Tigridias will not tolerate prolonged frost, so in cold areas lift in autumn and store in dry sand in a frost-free place. Propagate from seed sown in spring or by separating offsets when dormant. They are one of the quickest bulbs to flower from seed.

Hardiness Half hardy/Z8

Related plants T. vanhouttei has bronze-purple, stripy flowers, while T. durangense has dainty, lilac flowers.

Tulipa sprengeri (AGM)
Tulip
Origins: Turkey

One of the last tulips to flower, T. sprengeri has small, elegant scarlet flowers. It was collected in Turkey by Manissaadjian for the bulb firm Van Tubergen before the First World War, but it is said not to have been found in the wild since. It is a robust plant, and will happily self-seed and naturalize in meadows or light woodland.

Height 45–60cm (18–24in); **spread** 10–15cm (4–6in)

Cultivation Grow in any fertile, well-drained soil, preferably in full sun (T. sprengeri prefers more organic matter in the soil). Plant at a depth of around 10–15cm (4–6in) in late summer or autumn.

Hardiness Fully hardy/Z7

Related plants The fragrant, yellow flowers of T. sylvestris look best naturalized in grass. Low-growing T. biflora has starry, white flowers with yellow centres. Of the huge range of tulips available, those known as 'cottage tulips' (or, more prosaically, single, late tulips) are usually the simple-shaped forms in plain colours. They usually arose as 'cast-offs' from the highly prized florists' tulips. T. 'Advance' is flame-red and T. 'Golden Harvest' a deep lemon-yellow. T. 'Queen of Night' has lustrous, near-black petals. Of the robust Darwin hybrids, cherry-red T. 'Apeldoorn' is one of the most widely planted.

Other recommended bulbs
- *Allium rosenbachianum* (ornamental onion)
- *Scilla peruviana* (Peruvian scilla)

ABOVE: *The red heads and long stems of* Tulipa sprengeri *add a vibrant and animated splash of scarlet to woodland plantings.*

annuals & biennials
Generally easy to grow and fast to flower, annuals and biennials are ideal for bringing colour to new gardens. Many species can be encouraged to self-seed around the garden to give the informal feel that is perhaps the most typical image of the cottage garden.

ABOVE: **Alcea rosea** *produces tall spires of trumpet-shaped flowers.*

Height 1.5–2m (5–6½ft); **spread** 60cm (2ft)
Cultivation Sow seed on a windowsill or in a cold frame in late winter or outside in early spring. Pot plants up individually and plant out when young, as plants form a deep taproot. Hollyhocks prefer fertile soil in a sunny position.
Hardiness Fully hardy/Z5
Related plants *A. ficifolia*, the fig-leaved hollyhock from Siberia, has soft lemon flowers. It is less susceptible to rust than *A. rosea*. Perennial *Althaea officinalis* has soft, hairy leaves and pale pink flowers.

Calendula officinalis (AGM)
Pot marigold, English marigold
Origins: S. Europe to N. Africa
These fast-growing annuals have daisy-like flowers, usually orange, although there are cultivars in a range of colours including yellow cream and apricot. Selections with double flowers or with quilled petals are popular. The hen and chickens marigold (*C. officinalis* var. *prolifera*) has curious flowers in which the main flowerhead is surrounded by a ring of smaller ones. *Calendula* petals can be used to add colour to summer salads.

Height and spread Tall: 60cm (24in) × 60cm (24in); Dwarf: 30cm (12in) × 30cm (12in)
Cultivation The chunky seeds grow easily from a spring or autumn sowing where they are to flower. Marigolds will grow happily even in a poor soil, in sun or partial shade. Plants will self-seed generously unless deadheaded.
Hardiness Fully hardy/Z6
Related plants The French marigold (*Tagetes patula*) and the African marigold (*T. erecta*) are both native to Mexico. They are grown as bedding plants, giving long-lasting displays of colourful flowers. French marigolds have a pungent smell and are often used as companion plants to repel whitefly from tomatoes.

Digitalis purpurea (AGM)
Foxglove, Witch's bell, Thimbles
Origins: Europe
With beautiful spires of tubular flowers, often spotted inside, foxgloves are woodland biennials. The wild plant is usually rich purplish-pink, but *D. p. f. albiflora* has pure white flowers with variable amounts of spotting inside. 'Sutton's Apricot' is a soft apricot-pink. The plants are highly toxic.

Alcea rosea
Hollyhock
Origins: W. Asia
These traditional cottage-garden plants, with their stately spires of flowers, are often planted by doorways. During the 1840s and 1850s, William Chater grew an acre of hollyhocks at his nursery in Saffron Walden, England, producing richly coloured exhibition plants.

He is still remembered through the popular Chater's double seed strain, which has large, powder-puff flowers. Sadly, rust disease wiped out most of the Victorian hybrids and, today, hollyhocks are usually grown as biennials to reduce the effects of this disease. 'Majorette' is a bushy dwarf strain and 'Nigra' is popular for its dark, almost black, flowers.

ABOVE: **Calendula officinalis**

ABOVE: **Digitalis** *'Spice Island'*

Height 1–1.5m (39in–5ft); **spread** 60cm (2ft)
Cultivation Sow seed in late spring. Prick out when large enough to handle, then plant in the flowering position in late summer. Foxgloves look most natural in the dappled shade under trees. When happy they will self-seed profusely. Purple-flowered plants can be recognized as seedlings by the brownish or pale purple midribs on the leaves.
Hardiness Fully hardy/Z4
Related plants *D. lutea* is usually perennial with slender stems of small, soft lemon flowers. It seeds generously in alkaline soil. The rusty foxglove (*D. ferruginea*) has unusual, golden brown flowers on spikes 1.2–2m (4–6½ft) tall. The similarly coloured recent introduction *D.* 'Spice Island' is an evergreen foxglove.

Helianthus annuus (AGM)
Sunflower
Origins: USA and C. America
An annual used in religious ceremonies by the Incas and a favourite with artists, particularly during the Art Nouveau period, the sunflower is impossible to ignore. Tall cultivars such as 'Russian Giant' can reach heights of 4m (12ft) or more and have flowers to 25cm (10in) across. They are often grown by children in competitions for the tallest plant. 'Teddy Bear' is 1m (3ft) tall, with pompom-like, orange-yellow flowers. 'Music Box' gives multi-headed plants with colourful, often bi-coloured flowers.

ABOVE: **Papaver rhoeas**

Height to 5m (15ft); **spread** 30–45cm (12–18in)
Cultivation Sow seed in a cold frame in late winter or outdoors in spring. Sunflowers prefer full sun and a moderately fertile soil.
Hardiness Fully hardy/Z5
Related plants *H. debilis*, which originates from Florida and Texas, has nodding flowers, which, in the cultivar 'Italian White', are creamy white with a black central disc. *Rudbeckia hirta* is a biennial or short-lived perennial, usually grown as an annual. Commonly known as black-eyed Susan, it has daisy-like flowers in yellow or shades of bronze and gold, with dark eyes.

Nigella damascena (AGM)
Love-in-a-mist, Love-entangled, Devil-in-a-bush, Lady-in-the-bower, Bluebeard
Origins: S. Europe, N. Africa
An easy-to-grow annual with finely divided leaves and sapphire flowers. The inflated seed capsules contain black seeds, which give the plant its botanical name, *nigella* being a diminutive of *niger*, which means "black". *N.* 'Miss Jekyll' has sky-blue flowers. The Persian Jewel Series includes white, blue, violet and pink flowers. 'Blue Midget' is a dwarf, from just 25cm (10in) tall.
Height 60cm (24in); **spread** 20cm (8in)
Cultivation Sow seeds in spring where they are to flower in any well-drained soil in full sun. Sow in succession every three weeks to maintain colour all summer. Plants will self-seed generously, but seedlings are easily removed if unwanted.
Hardiness Fully hardy/Z5
Related plants *N. orientalis* 'Transformer' is a bushy plant with yellow flowers, usually grown for the odd, ribbed seedpods. The seeds of *N. sativa* are used as a flavouring in Middle Eastern cookery. Known as black cumin, they have a slightly bitter, oregano-like taste.

Papaver rhoeas
Common field poppy, Corn poppy, Flanders poppy
Origins: Eurasia, N. Africa
Blood-red field poppies have been associated with life and death, harvest and fertility for much of human history. The wild species with translucent,

ABOVE: *Nigella damascena growing with sedums and hardy geraniums.*

flame-red petals is lovely, but many selections are grown. One red poppy edged in white, selected by Victorian clergyman Rev. Wilkes of Shirley in Surrey, England, led to the range of Shirley poppies which have single flowers in many colours, all with pale centres. Artist-gardener Sir Cedric Morris raised the selection 'Mother of Pearl', known for its soft shades of pink, lilac and dove-grey.
Height 60cm (2ft); **spread** 30cm (1ft)
Cultivation Sow seed in autumn or early spring where it is to flower in a sunny spot with well-drained soil.
Hardiness Fully hardy/Z5
Related plants While sap from the unripened seedpods of *P. somniferum* is the source of opium, the seeds themselves do not contain toxins and so can be used to decorate bread. The opium poppy has blue-green leaves

and large flowers in mauve, red, pink, white or near-black. The peony-flowered or double forms give a traditional feel to borders. 'Hen and Chickens' has very large seedpods surrounded by smaller capsules.

Other recommended annuals and biennials
Annuals
- *Antirrhinum majus* (snapdragon) (AGM)
- *Centaurea cyanus* (cornflower)
- *Consolida ajacis* (larkspur)
- *Cosmos bipinnatus* (cosmos) (AGM)
- *Matthiola incana* (stocks)

Biennials
- *Dianthus barbatus* (sweet William) (AGM)
- *Erysimum cheiri*, syn. *Cheiranthus cheiri* (wallflower) (AGM)
- *Hesperis matronalis* (sweet rocket)

half-hardy & tender plants

This group of plants includes some with flamboyant colours or exotic scents which add excitement to the summer cottage garden. Many can be overwintered in a frost-free potting shed or garage if kept dryish at the root. Alternatively, take cuttings in late summer.

Argyranthemum frutescens (AGM)
Marguerite, Paris daisy, Atlantic Island daisy
Origins: Canary Islands
The marguerite has a very long flowering season, from late spring to late autumn, and long stems, which make the flowers good for cutting. Hybrids were developed between this species and relatives, including *A. foeniculaceum* and *A. gracile*. Many of the newer, compact hybrids, mostly bred in Australia, are known as Cobbitty daisies.
Height and spread 1m (39in)
Cultivation Propagate from semi-ripe cuttings taken in summer and overwintered on a windowsill. Plants are easily grown as standards by tying the main stem to a cane and pinching out any sideshoots. Once the stem reaches around 1m (39in), allow further sideshoots to develop. An impressive standard plant can be produced in 18 months to 2 years.
Hardiness Half hardy/Z10
Related plants *A.* 'Jamaica Primrose' is a bushy plant with single, lemon-yellow flowers. *A.* 'Cornish Gold' is similar, but with a denser habit. Pale pink, anemone-centred *A.* 'Mary Wootton'

is easy to train as a standard. *A.* 'Gypsy Rose' has single, carmine flowers and 'Ping Pong' is white with a dainty pompom-centred form.

Dahlia merckii
Dahlia
Origins: Mexico
One of the hardiest of dahlias, *D. merckii* forms a large plant when established, with stems bearing many nodding, purple, pink or white flowers. It blooms continuously from early summer through to autumn.
Height 1m (39in); **spread** 50cm (20in)
Cultivation *D. merckii* is a trouble-free perennial that is very easy to grow. With most dahlias, plant the tubers out in spring or start off in pots, planting out in early summer. Grow in a sheltered site with fertile, well-drained soil. In mild gardens, dahlias may survive over winter in the ground, but it is worth rooting some cuttings as a precaution against winter losses.
Hardiness Frost hardy/Z7
Related plants *D.* 'Bishop of Llandaff' has scarlet flowers and attractive, bronze foliage. The Collerette Group of cultivars has open-centred flowers. *D.* 'Clair de Lune' has yellow outer petals with an inner circle of pale lemon. *D.* 'Easter Sunday' is creamy white. Free-flowering *D.* 'Chimborazo' has deep red petals surrounding a frilly, yellow centre.

Heliotropium arborescens (AGM)
Heliotrope, Cherry Pie
Origins: Peru
Heliotrope is a bushy shrub with deep green, textured leaves. In frost-free gardens, the plants can be grown as headily scented hedges. In temperate areas, however, they are usually grown in containers. Most heliotrope flowers are in shades of mauve or purple. 'Marine' forms a compact plant with deep purple flowers. 'White Lady' is a silvery form.
Height and spread 1.5m (5ft)

ABOVE: Argyranthemum frutescens *produces masses of daisy-like flowers.*

Cultivation Usually grown as a half-hardy annual with seed sown under cover in early spring. Pot on and plant out after all risk of frost is past. Grow in a rich, moist soil with good protection from frosts. Semi-ripe cuttings root easily in summer.
Hardiness Half hardy/Z10
Related plants The Chatham Island forget-me-not (*Myosotidium hortensia*) is not closely related to heliotrope, but the flowers are similar. It is an

evergreen perennial with glossy, hosta-like leaves and ethereal, sky-blue flowers with darker centres.

Mirabilis jalapa
Four o'clock flower, Marvel of Peru, Belle de nuit
Origins: Tropical S. America
This tuberous perennial, which is usually grown as an annual, has colourful flowers shaped like miniature hunting horns. They are richly coloured and very fragrant,

ABOVE: Heliotropium arborescens

opening in late afternoon and dying by morning. These plants are fascinating because they often produce differently coloured flowers on a single plant, some plain and others distinctly striped.
Height 60cm–1.2m (2–4ft); spread 60–75cm (24–30in)
Cultivation Sow the chubby seeds under cover in early spring, planting out when all danger of frosts has passed. Grow in a well-drained soil in full sun. Plants are resistant to drought and heat, but require protection from slugs. In frost-prone areas, lift the fleshy tubers in autumn and store until spring.
Hardiness Frost hardy/Z8

Related plants *M. longiflora*, a native of Texas and Mexico, is a white-flowered species. The sand verbena (*Abronia wootonii*) has winged seeds that produce a tuberous plant, bearing clusters of fragrant, pink flowers. It requires a very free-draining soil and hot summers.

Pelargonium (Scented-leaved Group)
Geranium
Origins: S. Africa
Traditionally seen on the cottage windowsill, the scented-leaved geraniums are much-loved plants. *P.* 'Graveolens' of gardens, the rose geranium, has slightly rough, lobed

ABOVE: **Mirabilis jalapa**

ABOVE: **Pelargonium** *'Graveolens'*

leaves that can be used to make teas and jellies, while its oil is used in cosmetics and food flavourings. The apple geranium (*P. odoratissimum*) is short with a distinct apple fragrance. *P.* 'Mabel Grey' has purplish flowers and one of the strongest lemon scents. *P.* 'Chocolate Peppermint' has handsome leaves, with bronze centres and the fragrance of sweet peppermints.
Height 25–100cm (10–39in); spread 20–75cm (8–30in)
Cultivation Grow in a loam-based potting mix in full light. Water moderately and keep fairly dry over winter. To propagate, take softwood cuttings from spring to autumn.
Hardiness Frost tender/Z9
Related plants Zonal pelargoniums have more showy flowers, and rounded leaves with zones of different shades of green, yellow, bronze or maroon. *P.* 'Charlotte Brontë' has salmon-pink flowers and leaves that are yellow, green and red. Ivy-leaved pelargoniums, such as the old, variegated cultivar *P.* 'L'Elégante', are used to cascade out of window boxes.

Petunia Surfinia Series (AGM)
Petunia
Origins: Of garden origin
There are some 40 wild species of petunia in South America, but the popular garden plants are mostly derived from *P. violacea*, *P. axillaris* and *P. integrifolia*. The Surfinias have cascades of large, velvety flowers. The individual flowers only last a

day or so, but plants are very free-flowering and better able to resist wet weather than many other petunias. *P.* 'Priscilla', with richly scented, lavender-coloured flowers, is one of the Tumbelina Series of frilly, double cultivars.
Height 15–30cm (6–12in); spread 30cm (12in)
Cultivation Grow in a loam-based potting mix in full sun with shelter from inclement weather. Deadhead to prolong flowering. Propagate from seed sown in mid-spring or by rooting softwood cuttings. Some cultivars are protected by patents and may only be propagated under licence. Petunias are prone to a range of viruses.
Hardiness Half hardy/Z10
Related plants The velvet trumpet flower (*Salpiglossis sinuate*) is an erect annual, growing to 60cm (24in). The intensely coloured flowers have a velvety texture. Seed-raised plants give a selection of rich colours, including some with exotic veining in the centre. 'Casino Mixed' gives compact, profusely flowering plants in a rainbow of colours. 'Kew Blue' is a beautiful, royal purple.

Other recommended half-hardy and tender plants
- *Fuchsia* Shadow Dancer Series 'Rosella'
- *Osteospermum* Serenity Series 'Lemonade'
- *Verbena* Aztec Magic Series 'Purple Magic' (AGM)

ABOVE: **Petunia** *Surfinia Series plants are displayed here with* **Calibrachoa.**

plants for ponds

If you have a pond in your cottage garden, you can help to create a healthy ecosystem by growing a balanced selection of marginal (emergent) and submerged or deep-water plants. Avoid introducing invasive species such as parrot feather (*Myriophyllum spicatum*), which can get out of control.

Aponogeton distachyos
Water hawthorn, Cape pondweed
Origins: South Africa

The water hawthorn is frost hardy and may be evergreen in mild winters. It has bright green, oblong leaves, about 20cm (8in) long, and clusters of small, white, waxy flowers. The main flowering is in spring, but a second flush will occur in autumn.

Spread 1.2m (4ft)
Cultivation Grow in water 30–90cm (12–36in) deep, planting either in an aquatic planting basket or in the pond soil. Flowering is best in full sun, but plants tolerate dappled shade, so can be a good solution for shady ponds. In areas with very hard winters, lift the plants in autumn and store in a frost-free place until spring.

ABOVE: **Aponogeton distachyos**

ABOVE: **Nymphaea alba**

Propagate by division of the rhizomes when dormant.
Hardiness Frost hardy/Z7
Related plants Arrowhead (*Sagittaria sagittifolia*) produces round tubers that are popular with ducks. The flowers have three white petals, centred by purple stamens. There is a double-flowered plant, 'Flore Pleno'. It is an invasive cultivar in many states of America.

Caltha palustris (AGM)
Marsh marigold, Kingcup, Gold knobs, Butter clocks, Hobble-gobble, Marybuds
Origins: Northern temperate regions

A plant of moist meadows and wet woods, with deep green leaves and lacquered-yellow flowers in late winter in mild seasons, the marsh marigold is resistant to cold and wind. The white-flowered *C. p.* var. *alba* and the double 'Flore Pleno', with neat, frilly rosettes, are both more compact than the species. The North American *C. p.* var. *palustris* (syn. *C. polypetala* of gardens) has flowers that are up to 8cm (3in) across.
Height 23cm (9in); **spread** 30cm (12in)
Cultivation Best grown as a marginal aquatic in very shallow water or bog

conditions. It will grow in partial shade, but the flowers glow better in sun. Divide plants in late summer to increase stock. Handling the plant may cause skin irritations, so wear gloves.
Hardiness Fully hardy/Z3
Related plants The water crowfoot (*Ranunculus aquatilis*) is a useful oxygenating plant in water up to 1m (39in) deep. It has kidney-shaped, floating leaves and thread-like, submerged leaves. The buttercup-shaped flowers are white with a yellow centre.

Eriophorum angustifolium
Cotton grass, Bog cotton
Origins: N. Europe, N. America

A marginal aquatic plant with long, grass-like leaves and tassels of downy, white flowers in summer. The cotton-like fibres are too short to make a useable thread, but have been used for stuffing pillows and making candlewicks. Used for wound dressings in wartime.
Height 30cm (1ft); **spread** indefinite
Cultivation Grow at the margin of a pond to a water depth of not more than 5cm (2in) or in a bog garden. It requires an acid, peaty soil in full sun. Propagate by dividing established clumps.

ABOVE: **Eriophorum angustifolium** *is characterized by distinctive white tufts.*

ABOVE: Caltha palustris *is a member of the buttercup family.*

Hardiness Fully hardy/Z4

Related plants The sweet galingale (*Cyperus longus*) is one of only a few hardy members of a large genus that includes the Egyptian giant papyrus (*C. papyrus*). It has stiff, triangular stems, to 1.5m (5ft) tall, and loose umbels of red-brown flowers in late summer and autumn. It is vigorous and best kept in a planting basket. The umbrella grass (*C. alternifolius*) has stems to around 80cm (32in), topped with foliage arranged like the spokes of an umbrella. In mild areas, it can be grown outside all year round; alternatively, grow in a tub and keep in a frost-free place over winter. *C. glaber* is hardy with decorative flower spikelets.

Juncus effusus
Soft rush, Bog rush
Origins: Northern temperate regions

The soft rush has glossy, cylindrical stems, containing white pith. Rush lights, made by soaking lengths of peeled rush in hot fat, were the main source of light in most cottages up to the 19th century. Clusters of small, brown flowers are produced throughout summer. The corkscrew rush (*J. effusus* f. *spiralis*) is grown for its ornamental, densely spiralled stems. Variegated forms include 'Yellow Line' and 'Limelight'.

Height 1m (39in); **spread** 60cm (24in)

Cultivation Grow as a marginal plant in acid soil with a water depth of up to 12cm (5in) over the crown.

Plants prefer full sun. Propagate by division in spring.

Hardiness Fully hardy/Z2

Related plants The hard rush (*J. inflexus*) has prominently ridged, greyish green stems. It flowers earlier than *J. effusus* and grows well in heavy, alkaline soil. The cultivar 'Afro' has spiralled stems.

Nymphaea alba
Water lily
Origins: Eurasia, N. Africa

Widespread in lakes, ponds and slow-moving rivers, this water lily has showy, creamy white flowers. It is a vigorous plant and so is best planted only in larger ponds. A wild red form came from Tiveden in Sweden and has been much used in hybridization programmes.

Suggested planting depth 60cm (2ft); **spread** 2m (6½ft) or more

Cultivation Grow in still water in full sun. Plant the rhizomes in firm, loamy soil and cover with pea gravel. Contain in an aquatic planting basket to restrict vigour. Submerge freshly planted containers so that around 25cm (10in) of water covers the crown. Gradually increase the water depth to 60cm (2ft).

Hardiness Fully hardy/Z5

Related plants *N. tetragona* 'Helvola' (syn. 'Pygmaea Helvola') is the best water lily for small ponds or tubs. It has mottled leaves, 12cm (5in) long, and produces lemon-yellow, lightly fragrant flowers. *N.* 'Pygmaea Rubra' has deep pinkish-red

flowers. *N.* 'Joanne Pring' is a miniature, pink-flowering cultivar with leaves around 5cm (2in) in diameter.

Typha minima
Miniature bulrush, Reedmace, Cat's tail
Origins: Eurasia

This slender relative of the bulrush is suitable for half barrels, patio pots or small ponds. In mid- to late summer, it produces ornamental spikes of dark brown flowers. The cylindrical flowerheads can be picked early in the season for drying, but should be sealed with hair spray.

Height 45–60cm (18–24in); **spread** 30cm (12in)

Cultivation Grow in a water depth of around 10cm (4in) in full sun. Plant in an aquatic planting basket, using a loamy soil. Propagate by dividing the rootstock in spring.

Hardiness Fully hardy/Z5

Related species The most common species, *T. latifolia*, is a vigorous plant, with leaves to 2.5m (8ft) tall, and should only be planted in the largest wildlife ponds. The rhizomes have sharp tips and can puncture pond liners. 'Variegata' is rather slower growing, with leaves striped in cream and green. It reaches around 1.2m (4ft) in height.

Other recommended pond plants
- *Eichornia crassipes* (water hyacinth)
- *Iris laevigata* 'Variegata' (Japanese water iris) (AGM)

ABOVE: Juncus effusus

ABOVE: Typha minima

fruit & nuts
Needing little attention, fruit bushes and fruit and nut trees remain a productive part of the cottage garden for many years. Looking at fruit and then at nuts, this shows a small selection of the choices in both categories. Most nut trees crop better if grown with a different clone to cross-pollinate.

Fragaria x *ananassa* (AGM)
Strawberry
Origins: Of garden origin
Garden strawberries have been bred mainly from American wild species, including *F. virginiana* and *F. chiloensis*. 'Royal Sovereign' has a good flavour, but is susceptible to virus disease. 'Pegasus' is one of the best late-season cultivars. 'Aromel' is an ever-bearer that begins to fruit in early summer and continues until autumn.
Cultivation Choose a warm, sunny situation on well-drained, ideally slightly acid, soil. Water regularly and when fruits start to form put a thick layer of straw or proprietary matting underneath to keep the berries clean. Net the ripening fruit to protect them.
Potential problems Birds and slugs are the two worst problems. Net the plants while they are in fruit. Burn and destroy plants with viral diseases and grey mould.
Hardiness Fully hardy/Z5
Related plants The European wild or woodland strawberry (*F. vesca*) has small fruits that are easily bruised, but are very flavourful. Seed-raised alpine strawberries, such as 'Mignonette', produce small, sweet, aromatic berries.

ABOVE: **Malus sylvestris** *var.* domestica

Malus sylvestris var. *domestica* (AGM)
Apple
Origins: Of garden origin
More than 6,000 cultivars of apple have been bred, of which probably a third survive. 'Lord Lambourne', 'Egremont Russet' and 'St Edmund's Pippin' are good, mid-season apples that will cross-pollinate each other. 'Ashmead's Kernel' and 'D'Arcy Spice' are well-flavoured, late-season cultivars.
Cultivation Easily grown in all but tropical and subtropical regions. A sunny, sheltered site is best with a well-drained soil. Apples are generally grafted on to a rootstock – choose the one with the ultimate height that you have room for. You will need at least two compatible trees to ensure pollination.
Potential problems Birds, wasps and codling moths are significant pests and canker one of the worst diseases.
Hardiness Fully hardy/Z3–8

Prunus domestica (AGM)
Plum
Origins: Of garden origin
Plums make excellent trees with spring blossom followed by a harvest of fruits. 'Victoria' is the most common cultivar, but there are numerous others. 'Impérial Epineuse' has soft, juicy, well-flavoured fruits. 'Marjorie's Seedling' is a late cultivar that shows resistance to canker.
Cultivation Plant in a sheltered site, avoiding frost pockets. Most cultivars are at least partially self-fertile, but planting suitable pollinators nearby will ensure a reliable crop. Thinning the fruit will give larger individual fruits, and reduce the risk of branches breaking.
Potential problems Pests include birds, rabbits, wasps, aphids and winter moths. Burn or destroy trees affected by silver leaf, canker and brown rot.
Hardiness Fully hardy/Z4–9
Related plants Greengages, developed from a green-fruited, wild plum, have a rich, sweet taste. Damsons (*P. domestica* subsp. *insititia*) are small, black plums

that make superb jellies and jams. The 'Mirabelle' is a golden yellow plum that grows well in warm areas.

Pyrus communis var. *sativa* (AGM)
Pear
Origins: Of garden origin
The French first popularized pears in the Middle Ages. The best eating pears, such as 'Beth' and 'Doyenné du Comice', are richly flavoured and meltingly sweet. Culinary pears, like the ancient warden pear *P.* 'Warden' are delicious when poached in cider or wine.
Cultivation Pears require rather warmer conditions than apples and are often grown trained against a wall to benefit from the extra warmth and shelter. Most pears are grafted on to a quince rootstock to produce a manageable tree and to induce early fruiting.
Potential problems Problems include pests, such as aphids and pear midge, and diseases such as canker and brown rot. Pears affected by fireblight must be destroyed.
Hardiness Fully hardy/Z4–9
Related plants Quinces (*Cydonia oblonga*) have large, fragrant apple- or pear-shaped fruits, not eaten raw but used to add flavour to other cooked fruits. They are covered in a whitish down. The trees have large blossoms in spring, and are widely grown in southern Europe where hot summers ensure the fruit ripens.

Ribes uva-crispa (AGM)
Gooseberry, Goosegogs
Origins: N. E. and C. Europe
Gooseberries were developed from the wild plant, a spiny bush with small, hairy berries. By late Victorian times, more than 2,000 cultivars were grown and gooseberry clubs flourished. Most commercial gooseberries are green and tart, but there are many with sweet dessert fruits in yellow, red or black. 'Yellow Champagne' (syn. 'Hairy Amber') is one of the best for flavour with small,

ABOVE: *Pyrus communis* var. *sativa*

yellow, hairy berries. 'Ironmonger' is a richly flavoured, dark red cultivar. 'Hero of the Nile' has sweet, yellow berries.
Cultivation Grow in well-drained soil and mulch to keep roots cool. Will fruit reliably in sun or partial shade. Usually grown as a goblet-shaped bush, but may also be trained as a standard or as cordons or fans against a wall or along wires. Propagate from hardwood cuttings taken in autumn.
Potential problems Gooseberries are not prone to many pests and diseases. To prevent powdery mildew, ensure there is plenty of air circulation. In spring, birds may also strip off buds.
Hardiness Fully hardy/Z4–7
Related plants The jostaberry (*R. nidigrolaria*) is a hybrid between the gooseberry and the blackcurrant. The fruit resembles a blackcurrant, but is twice the size. It makes a vigorous, thornless bush that shows good resistance to American gooseberry mildew and several other diseases.

Other recommended fruit
- *Rheum* x *hybridum* (rhubarb)
- *Ribes nigrum* (blackcurrant) (AGM)
- *Rubus fruticosus aggregate* (blackberry) (AGM)

ABOVE: Corylus avellana

ABOVE: Castanea sativa 'Variegata'

Castanea sativa
Sweet or Spanish chestnut
Origins: Asia Minor, North Africa and Southern Europe

Chestnut trees can grow to be as much as 30m (100ft) tall, so need a large garden. They like at least a moderately warm climate and a light and well-drained soil in full sun. The cultivar 'Regal' is more compact than others, reaching around 5m (15ft) in ten years. The shiny, rich brown nuts are superb straight from the tree or can be roasted or used in stuffings. Marron-type chestnuts, such as 'Marron de Lyon', have large, single nuts, whereas the wild-type châtaignes have multiple nuts in a case.

Cultivation Plant initially in a container then early to a permanent position, and prune to create a strong shape.

Hardiness Fully hardy/Z4–8

Corylus avellana
Hazel, Ranger, Cob
Origins: Europe and Turkey

A well-known shrub with 'lamb's-tail' catkins in late winter, hazel has been used since Neolithic times as wattle to make fencing and wattle-and-daub walls. Hazelnuts have been grown in cottage gardens since at least the 15th century and probably earlier. They are grown as open-centred bushes, with any but the best-placed, strongest shoots removed to develop a good framework. The nuts are delicious. 'Cosford Cob' is still one of the most popular. Plants make excellent productive hedges and are invaluable

coppiced to provide stakes for the garden, firewood, walking sticks and the hazel pegs used by thatchers.

Cultivation Likes a well-drained and loamy soil. Plant more than one variety (to allow cross-pollination) in a sheltered position in dappled shade. Established bushes fruit better if the longer sideshoots are broken along their length in late summer and left to hang, called 'brutting', a technique that encourages the production of female flowers. Happy through cold, wet winter conditions.

Potential problems These plants have few problems, with the exception of squirrels that steal the nuts.

Hardiness Fully hardy/Z3

Related plants Cobnuts (*C. avellana*) and filberts (*C. maxima*) are usually both called hazels, and crop best in cool, moist summers. They both produce male catkins and tiny female flowers in late winter, and are wind-pollinated. There are a number of self-fertile cultivars, but even these will give a better crop if you grow more than one clone.

Recommended cultivars of cobnuts include 'Cosford' and 'Nottingham', both popular and self-fertile. 'Butler' is a vigorous selection from the United States, which gives a heavy crop of large nuts. The Italian 'Tonda di Giffoni' has large, thin-shelled nuts. The trazel (*C. x colurnoides*) is a cross between the common hazel and the Turkish tree hazel (*C. colurna*). It is usually trained as a standard tree, which can make the crop easier to protect from squirrels.

Corylus maxima
Filbert
Origins: Asia Minor

Filberts are distinguished from cobnuts by the husk, which is longer than the nut and may completely enclose it. 'Frizzled Filbert' has ornamental, frilled husks. The purple filbert 'Purpurea' has copper foliage and makes an excellent ornamental hedge. The cultivar 'Kentish Cob', which is actually a filbert, was introduced in around 1830 and is still one of the most widely grown.

Cultivation As *C. avellana* (above).

Potential problems As *C. avellana* (above).

Hardiness Fully hardy/Z3

Juglans regia
Walnut
Origins: Persia

The walnut can be susceptible to frost damage in cold sites. The trees may be slow to establish, but can eventually reach heights of around 18m (60ft) in favourable positions. The old French cultivar 'Franquette' is a reliable plant. 'Rita' forms a small tree, and is both hardy and productive. The Bulgarian 'Proslavski' is vigorous with large nuts. The heartnut or Japanese walnut (*J. ailantifolia*) is reputed to be easier to

grow than walnuts. It is hardy to around -25°C (-13°F) on a sunny site in heavy, free-draining yet moisture-retentive soil. Two clones are required for cross-pollination.

Cultivation Walnuts should be transplanted as young trees as they grow quickly and older specimens don't like being moved. When planting permanently, incline the tree slightly towards prevailing winds. Stake the tree for a minimum of two years.

Hardiness Fully hardy/Z3–7

Prunus dulcis
Almonds
Origins: Middle East and South Asia

Almonds are ornamental trees with attractive, pink blossom. Most varieties are suitable only for frost-free areas with warm, dry summers, but newer cultivars such as 'Mandaline' do not flower until mid-spring and will grow in cold areas if the flowers escape the frosts. 'Robijn' and the old French cultivar 'Ardechoise' are soft-shelled nuts.

Cultivation Prefers a site in full sun and deep, moist, free-draining soil. Two trees are advisable for maximum pollination and cropping. Should produce nuts after 3 years.

Hardiness Fully hardy/Z7–9

ABOVE: *Juglans regia grows best in full sun on well-drained, fertile soil.*

vegetables

Even without a designated plot, many different vegetables can be grown in the cottage garden among the flowers in borders or in tubs, troughs and hanging baskets. There is something that is uniquely satisfying about using produce in the kitchen that you have grown and cared for yourself.

ABOVE: *Container-grown cabbages need plenty of water.*

Brassica oleracea Capitata Group (AGM)
Cabbage
Origins: Mediterranean

Probably the most important vegetable in the earliest cottage gardens, the cabbage was indispensable for winter soups. The old variety of Savoy cabbage, 'Filderkraut' from Germany, has huge, pointed heads that are traditionally used in coleslaw and sauerkraut.

Cultivation Most cabbages are grown as annuals. They are very hardy, with some cultivars surviving temperatures down to -10°C (14°F). Seed is usually sown in a seedbed or modules, with seedlings being transplanted around five weeks later. They need a fertile, moisture-retentive soil and firm planting. Most soils should be limed regularly.

Potential problems To deter cabbage root fly, place a collar aound the plant's stem. Cover plants with netting to deter caterpillar eggs. If club root occurs, destroy affected plants, do not plant any related plants in the site for 20 years, and avoid transferring soil on your boots.

Hardiness Fully hardy/Z3

Related plants Kale (*B. oleracea* Acephala Group) is the hardiest of the brassicas, and plants can stand a long time in the ground with leaves snapped off as required. 'Cottagers Kale' is a hardy, old variety with red-veined leaves. 'Nero di Toscana' is a kale/cabbage hybrid with oblong, crinkled leaves. Modern cultivars of Brussels sprouts (*B. oleracea* Gemmifera Group), such as 'Brigitte' and 'Breton', lack the bitterness associated with sprouts.

Daucus carota (AGM)
Carrot
Origins: Europe to India

The thick taproots of cultivated carrots were probably developed from the Mediterranean subspecies *sativus* of the wild carrot. White and pale yellow varieties were most common in Europe; purple carrots are believed to have originated in Afghanistan. It was Dutch growers in the 16th century who developed the orange carrot. The cultivar 'Early French Frame' has small, round roots and is good with heavy soils. 'Giant Flakkee' has large, richly coloured roots that store well. There is a white variety known as 'Belgian White'.

Cultivation Sow in succession from early spring, 1–2cm ($^1/_2$–$^3/_4$in) deep in rows 15cm (6in) apart. Choose an open site in light, fertile soil.

Potential problems Carrot flies are attracted to the plant's odour. To disguise the smell, plant garlic nearby. If carrot fly are a problem, surround the patch with a barrier of fine mesh netting, 60–90cm (2–3ft) high, or try companion planting with French marigolds (*Tagetes patula*). Many carrots suffer from violet root rot. Do not plant them on the affected ground for a couple of years.

Hardiness Fully hardy/Z3

Related plants Parsnips (*Pastinaca sativa*) are a useful winter vegetable.

The flavour of the root improves after frost and, except in severe winters, roots may be left in the ground until required. 'Tender and True' has a good flavour and is resistant to canker.

Lycopersicon esculentum (AGM)
Tomato
Origins: S. America

The tomato was an ancient food crop in South and Central America. Now it is one of the most widely grown vegetables with many forms. 'Silvery Fir Tree' has feathery foliage and good crops of medium-sized fruit. 'Black Russian' has richly flavoured, deep purple tomatoes. 'Garden Peach' has furry foliage and fruits with fuzzy skins.

Cultivation Sow seed indoors in spring in seed trays or modules. Pot up when seedlings have two or three leaves, then plant out when the first flowers are visible and all risk of frost has passed. Cordon type tomatoes such as 'Gardeners' Delight' and 'Mirabelle' need the sideshoots to be removed regularly to concentrate the plants' energy into fruiting. Bush tomatoes such as 'Pixie' and 'Plumito' can be allowed to sprawl.

ABOVE: **Daucus carota**

ABOVE: **L. esculentum** *(Tomato 'Sunbaby')*

Potential problems Possible pests are whitefly, aphids and potato cyst eelworm. Diseases include tomato blight and grey mould. French marigolds (*Tagetes patula*) can repel whitefly, and good ventilation deters mould. Blight is wind-borne – avoid it by growing under glass.
Hardiness Half hardy/Z7
Related plants Aubergines or eggplants (*Solanum melongena*) can be grown in much the same way as tomatoes, but usually require higher temperatures. Keep plants well watered to avoid bud drop. There is a great variety of shape and colour. The Italian 'Listada di Gandia' has fruits striped white and purple. 'Pingtung Long' has long, finger-like fruits.

Phaseolus coccineus (AGM)
Runner bean, Scarlet bean
Origins: C. America

An important crop in Inca and Aztec societies, the runner bean was first grown as an ornamental in Europe. Today, it is grown over arches or up a strong support of poles or canes. The runner bean is a perennial climber, grown as an annual in areas prone to frost. The flowers may be red, white, pink or bicoloured. The red-and-white flowered cultivar 'Painted Lady' was in cultivation by 1633.
Cultivation Sow seed *in situ* in a well-prepared, rich soil after all risk of frost has passed, or start off seeds indoors, hardening off the seedlings before transplanting. Water well, particularly as

ABOVE: **Pisum sativum**

flower buds start to appear. In hot climates, plants will grow better in shade.
Potential problems Although generally problem free, runner beans can be affected by slugs and snails (which appear as plants first emerge), and possible attacks of blackfly.
Hardiness Frost tender/Z10
Related plants French beans (*P. vulgaris*) have climbing and dwarf forms. 'Purple Teepee' is a dwarf form with stringless, purple pods that turn emerald green when boiled. The Italian climbing bean 'Barlotta lingua di fuoco' has red, marbled pods. A notable American variety is 'Cherokee Trail of Tears'.

Pisum sativum (AGM)
Peas
Origins: E. Mediterranean

Peas have been cultivated for consumption, both fresh and dried, for thousands of years. There are many cultivars, with plants ranging in sizes up to 2m (6½ft) tall. The old variety 'Half Pint' is just 30–40cm (12–15in) tall, and can be grown in a pot or window box.
Cultivation Grow in a fertile soil in a sunny position. Sow at fortnightly intervals from early spring. Protect young seedlings against birds with horticultural fleece or netting. Once plants start to produce tendrils, insert peasticks or canes to support the growing plants.
Potential problems To prevent birds stripping the emerging seedlings, it may be necessary to protect them with wire netting. Mildew is common, yet can be ignored.
Hardiness Fully hardy/Z5
Related plants Snow peas, often called mangetout or sugarsnap peas, have edible pods. Reliable cultivars include 'Garbon' and 'Oregon Pea'. 'Carouby de Maussane' is a vigorous, ornamental plant with purple-maroon flowers. The asparagus pea (*Lotus tetragonolobus*) has small, brilliant red flowers and winged pods that are best eaten when up to 3cm (1½in) long.

Solanum tuberosum (AGM)
Potato
Origins: Chile and Peru
The potato had been cultivated by pre-Inca nations in its South American homeland and so was an ancient crop long before it was introduced to

ABOVE: **Phaseolus coccineus** (runner bean) plants are decorative and highly productive.

Europe in the 16th century. Except in Ireland, it did not become common in cottage gardens until the late 18th century. By Victorian times, half of the area devoted to vegetables would be planted with potatoes. Recommended maincrop cultivars include 'King Edward' and 'Maris Piper'. The French cultivar 'Ratte' and 'Pink Fir Apple' are excellent in salads.
Cultivation Chit early potatoes indoors to start them into growth about six weeks before planting. Place tubers in an open box in a cool, light room. Plant out when shoots are around 2cm (¾in) long and risk of frost has passed. Potatoes must be earthed up to prevent tubers turning green. Early potatoes are harvested when the flowers start to open; maincrop potatoes can be left in the soil for longer.

Potential problems Potatoes are affected by blight and blackleg. For blight, do not plant potatoes on ground that was affected the year before. Look out for resistant varieties.
Hardiness Half hardy/Z4–9
Related plants Jerusalem artichokes (*Helianthus tuberosus*) are perennial plants in the sunflower family, usually characterized by very knobbly tubers. 'Fuseau' produces smooth, easy-to-peel tubers, with a distinctive, smoky flavour. Plant in any soil; they are easy-to-grow, hardy plants and may, indeed, be invasive once planted.

Other recommended vegetables
• *Allium cepa* (onion) (AGM)
• *Brassica olearacea* Botrytis Group (cauliflower) (AGM)
• *Vicia faba* (broad bean, fava bean)

herbs
Growing herbs has always been a fundamental part of cottage gardening because of their extensive culinary and medicinal uses. They are also highly ornamental and often have aromatic leaves. Including a selection of herbs will attract many beneficial insects to your garden.

Borago officinalis
Borage
Origins: Mediterranean

The pure blue, starry flowers of borage are best known for their use in the alcoholic drink Pimms. The cucumber-scented, rather bristly leaves can be used in salads, while plants grown from an autumn sowing are a popular vegetable in the Aragon region of Spain. In mild climates, borage will flower for much of the year and it is extremely popular with bees. The white-flowered form is pretty, but not as well loved as the normal form with its intense blue flowers.

Height 30–100cm (12–36in); **spread** 15–30cm (6–12in)

Cultivation Borage is an annual plant, usually grown from seed sown outdoors in spring. It is easy to grow in any reasonably drained soil and will often self-seed freely. Susceptible to powdery mildew in dry summers.

Hardiness Fully hardy/Z7

Related plants Comfrey (*Symphytum grandiflorum*) is a vigorous perennial with nodding, tubular flowers in creamy white, pink or various shades of purple. It grows freely in sun or dappled shade. Its leaves are often steeped in water to make an organic liquid fertilizer. The sterile Bocking 14 form will not seed madly all over the garden.

Lavandula angustifolia (AGM)
Lavender
Origins: W. Mediterranean

A bushy shrub with aromatic, grey-green leaves, lavender produces dense spikes of fragrant, purple flowers throughout summer, which are very attractive to bees and butterflies. Lavender is a popular, short hedging plant. The dried flowerheads are invaluable in pot-pourris, but can also be used in cooking. Lavender adds a wonderful aroma to roast lamb, while a teaspoon of the flowers gives an excellent flavour when stirred into shortbread mixtures.

Height 60–90cm (2–3ft); **spread** 60–120cm (2–4ft)

Cultivation Grow in well-drained soil in a sunny spot. Easy to grow from seed or by cuttings taken between late winter and autumn. Trim regularly to keep a compact shape.

Hardiness Fully hardy/Z5

Related plants The French lavender (*L. stoechas*) has dark purple flowers, topped by conspicuous bracts that look like rabbits' ears. It is attractive grown in pots. The cultivar 'Kew Red' has chubby, bright cerise flowers crested with pale pink bracts. *L. lanata*, the woolly lavender, has soft, silver-grey leaves.

Petroselinum crispum
Parsley
Origins: Middle East

Parsley is a hardy biennial with bright green, crinkled leaves that are popular as a garnish or pot herb. The curly leaved forms make pretty edging or container plants. If left to grow for a second season, it produces flat heads of greenish-yellow flowers. It is used as a companion plant to repel insect pests from crops such as tomatoes.

Height and spread 30cm (1ft)

Cultivation Sow seed at intervals from early spring to late summer. Parsley can be slow to germinate, often taking four to six weeks.

ABOVE: **Borago officinalis** *has edible flowers within hairy calyces.*

ABOVE: **Salvia officinalis**

ABOVE: **Petroselinum crispum**

Hardiness Frost hardy/Z6
Related plants *P. c.* var. *neopolitanum* is a flat-leaved parsley with a stronger flavour and higher levels of essential oils. The flat-leaved parsleys are hardier, more vigorous plants than the curly forms. The Hamburg root parsley (*P. crispum* var. *tuberosum*), grown for its turnip-like root, is a popular vegetable in Central and Eastern Europe.

Rosmarinus officinalis (AGM)
Rosemary
Origins: Mediterranean
Rosemary is an upright evergreen shrub, cultivated for its aromatic foliage and for the misty blue flowers, which are often borne very early in the year and continue for long periods. The leaves are used fresh or dried in cooking, and have a particular affinity with lamb. Rosemary is traditionally grown in the herb garden, but is a good plant for gravel gardens and can also be used for topiary as it responds well to clipping. 'Severn Sea' is a good, bright blue flowering cultivar with attractive, arching branches. 'Roseus' has pink flowers.
Height 1.5–1.8m (5–6ft);
spread 1.5m (5ft)
Cultivation Rosemary prefers full sun in a free-draining soil. In cold areas, grow against a sunny wall. Semi-ripe cuttings taken in summer will root easily in pots of gritty potting mix.
Hardiness Frost hardy/Z6
Related plants Hyssop (*Hyssopus officinalis*) is a semi-evergreen, dwarf

ABOVE: *Thymus vulgaris* **'Silver Posie'**

shrub with aromatic leaves and delicate spikes of blue flowers that are very attractive to bees and butterflies. Hyssop makes an excellent edging plant in the herb garden. It has a strong, camphor-like smell and was used as a strewing herb.

Salvia officinalis (AGM)
Common sage
Origins: Mediterranean and N. Africa
With soft, grey-green leaves and spikes of lilac-blue flowers, sage is an attractive plant in the flower border or rock garden, as well as the herb bed. The word *salvia* means "to heal", and the plant has been used for many medicinal purposes over the years. Sage can form a sprawling sub-shrub unless regularly clipped, but, as it is a popular culinary herb, regular picking of the leaves is no hardship. It is often used with onion to make savoury stuffings, and is much used in Italian cooking.
Height 60–75cm (24–30in); **spread** 60–90cm (2–3ft)
Cultivation Grow in a light, free-draining soil in full sun or semi-shade, although the most aromatic leaves will be produced with plenty of sun. Take cuttings in summer or early autumn.
Hardiness Fully hardy/Z5
Related plants There are a number of different colour-leaved forms of the common sage. The cultivar 'Aurea' is a more compact plant with yellow leaves and deeper coloured flowers. The purple sage, 'Purpurascens', makes a good contrast to the yellow form. 'Icterina' is a cultivar with yellow-and-green variegated leaves. 'Tricolor' has leaves that are edged with cream and emerge pinkish-purple.

Thymus vulgaris
Thyme
Origins: Mediterranean
Attractive to bees and indispensable in the kitchen, thyme is one of the most well loved culinary herbs. It has tiny, aromatic leaves and purple or white flowers. The cultivar 'Silver Posie' has leaves edged with white. Thyme is widely used to flavour meats, as well as soups and stews, and is a traditional component of the bouquet garni, much used in French cuisine.

Height 15–30cm (6–12in);
spread 40cm (16in)
Cultivation Thyme prefers a well-drained soil and will grow well on chalk. Choose a sunny position and cut plants back after flowering to keep them compact. Plants tolerate drought well. Propagate from cuttings taken any time during the summer.
Hardiness Fully hardy/Z7
Related plants Mat-forming *T. serpyllum* can be used for thyme carpets or to grow in gaps between paving. The different colour forms can be planted together to give a tapestry-like effect. The cultivar 'Pink Chintz' has greyish-green leaves and soft pink flowers. Lemon-scented *T. citriodorous* is particularly popular, and the yellow-leaved form, *T. pulegioides* 'Bertram Anderson', is a good edging plant.

Other recommended herbs
- Angelica (*Angelica archangelica*) is a tall architectural biennial with globular green flowerheads and hollow stems that can be candied.
- Sweet cicely (*Myrrhis odorata*) has pleasantly-scented fern-like leaves and is used to sweeten stewed fruits.
- Basil (*Ocimum basilicum*) is a tender plant usually grown as an annual. The pungent leaves combine brilliantly with tomato-based dishes.
- Bergamot (*Monarda didyma*) has aromatic leaves and striking crowns of flowers that are attractive to bees.
- Chives (*Allium schoenoprasum*) have a mild onion flavour.
- Mints such as *Mentha spicata* are popular and are often grown in sunken bottomless buckets as they can be invasive.

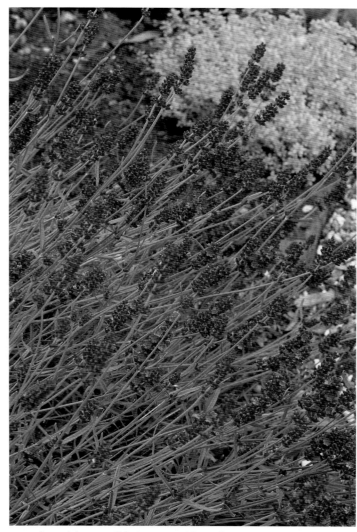

ABOVE: *Lavandula augustifolia* is an essential ingredient in pot-pourris.

collectors' plants

Because of the sheer variety of plants, cottage garden owners often have a collector's interest in a particular genus. Indeed, a group of plants from the same genetic group can make an interesting display, with small bulbs or perennials perhaps the easiest to present attractively.

Galanthus nivalis (AGM)
Snowdrop, Fair maids of February
Origins: Pyrenées to Ukraine

This snowdrop is a lovely plant for naturalizing in light woodland. Of the many named selections of *G. nivalis* itself, particularly treasured is *G. n.* f. *pleniflorus* 'Lady Elphinstone', which, when established, has double flowers with apricot-yellow markings. *G.* 'Robin Hood' is a robust hybrid with large flowers, the innermost petals of which have scissor-shaped marks. Of the yellow hybrids, *G.* 'Primrose Warburg' is especially good because established bulbs often produce two flower stems with tiny, pink blooms.
Height 10–15cm (4–6in); **spread** 5–8cm (2–3in)

Cultivation Snowdrops do not generally appreciate being grown in pots as they can dry out too much in summer. They grow best in moist but well-drained soil, which is rich in organic matter, in dappled shade. Split choice bulbs regularly to establish a supply of replacements should soil-living pests eat the bulbs.
Hardiness Fully hardy/Z4
Related plants Snowflakes, in the genera *Leucojum* and *Acis*, are similar to snowdrops, but the flowers have six equal petals. The summer snowflake (*L. aestivum*) is a tall plant, best grown beside a pond. *A. autumnalis* has white or pink-tinged bells from late summer. *A. rosea* flowers around the same time and has tiny, sugar-pink bells.

Hepatica nobilis var. japonica (AGM)
Hepatica
Origins: Japan

Cult plants in Japan, these come in an array of colours and forms. The European *H. nobilis* is an easy, but slow-growing, perennial that will self-seed to form an evergreen carpet in suitable conditions. It is less variable than the Japanese plant, but is available in shades of blue, pink and white, while double forms such as *H. n.* 'Rubra Plena' also exist.
Height 8cm (3in); **spread** 10–12cm (4–5in)
Cultivation Plants for display are usually grown in deep pots of potting mix, which is well-drained, but rich in organic matter. Keep plants cool and shaded after flowering. Propagate by division after flowering or in autumn for named cultivars. Seed-raised plants will be very variable.
Hardiness Fully hardy/Z5
Related plants *Adonis* have long been admired in Japan. *A.* 'Fukujukai' has large, golden yellow, semi-double flowers that emerge in late winter, surrounded by a ruff of ferny leaves. *A. multiflora* 'Sandanzaki' (syn. *A. amurensis* 'Pleniflora') has double flowers with 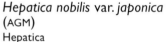 petals in three layers: first yellow, then green and, finally, yellow again. *A. amurensis* 'Chichibushinko' has flowers of a lovely copper colour.

Pelargonium (Unique Group)
Unique pelargonium, Unique geranium
Origins: Of garden origin

These large, shrubby pelargoniums have a very long flowering period. If protected from frost in winter, they will develop into spectacular flowering shrubs. Many Uniques have flowers in shades of red and are thought to have the species *P. fulgidum* in their ancestry. 'Paton's Unique' has aromatic leaves and deep coral-red flowers. 'Phyllis' is a sport of 'Paton's Unique' with green-and-gold variegated leaves.
Height over 40–45m (16–18in); **spread** 15–20cm (6–8in)
Cultivation Grow in a loam-based potting mix in good light. Prune the plant back by half each year to maintain a good bushy shape. Feed once a fortnight during the growing season with a high-potash, tomato-type fertilizer.
Hardiness Frost tender/Z9

ABOVE: Galanthus nivalis *are among the first spring bulb blooms to appear.*

ABOVE: Pelargonium *Unique Group*

ABOVE: Primula auricula *is a species of primrose, here shown in a spring border.*

ABOVE: Hepatica nobilis *'Indigo'*

ABOVE: Viola odorata

Related plants Angel pelargoniums are very bushy, small geraniums, possibly derived from *P. crispum*. The round, mid-green leaves are sometimes scented, but they are mainly grown for the profusion of pretty, regal-type flowers. The group name comes from their resemblance to an old plant from the 1820s called 'Angeline'. The group is currently popular, with many new introductions being made including the delightfully named 'Wayward Angel'.

Primula auricula (AGM)
Auricula, Bears' ears
Origins: Europe

One of the true florists' flowers, auricula breeding was popular among both the rich and artisan cottagers. Many cultivars, including those with exotic-coloured edges, striped petals and double flowers, were developed with strict rules laid down for show plants. Many cultivars were lost in the 20th century, but a recent revival of enthusiasm means that many of the more unusual forms are being recreated.
Height 20cm (8in); **spread** 25cm (10in)
Cultivation Border and alpine auriculas can be grown in the open garden in sun or partial shade. They need a reasonably fertile, moist, but well-drained, soil. Show auriculas have a mealy farina on the leaves and flowers, and must be protected from adverse weather in a cold frame, alpine house or other structure. Keep cool over summer.
Hardiness Fully hardy/Z3
Related plants There are a huge number of cultivated primulas, of which the gold-laced and double-flowered forms are most associated with cottage gardens. The soft, lilac, double-flowered *P. vulgaris* 'Lilacina Plena' is a very good, vigorous plant. Unusual forms such as hose-in-hose primulas, which have one flower sitting inside another, are still to be found.

Sempervivum tectorum (AGM)
Houseleek, Liveforever, Hen and Chicks
Origins: S. Europe

Houseleeks were traditionally grown on roofs to ward off lightning. *S. tectorum* and its relatives have given rise to numerous cultivars that are popular chiefly for their colourful rosettes of leaves. The cobweb houseleek (*S. arachnoideum*) has rosettes covered with cobweb-like hairs. *S. ciliosum*, which has very hairy rosettes, is best protected from winter wet.
Height 10–15cm (4–6in); **spread** 20cm (8in)
Cultivation Sempervivums are mostly easily grown, drought-tolerant plants. They will thrive in poor soil in full sun. Propagate by rooting the offsets, which are freely produced.
Hardiness Fully hardy/Z4
Related plants Jovibarbas are closely related, but have six-petalled, bell-like, yellow flowers, rather than the starry flowers of sempervivums. In mild climates, aeoniums make fantastic specimens with big, plate-like rosettes. *Aeonium* 'Zwartkop' forms a branched specimen with near-black leaves.

Viola odorata (AGM)
Sweet violet
Origins: W. and S. Europe

Sweet violets were used in perfumery in classical times and as a strewing herb in medieval Britain. The flowers are edible and can be candied as cake decorations. When crossed with the robust Russian species *V. suavis*, a range of large, vigorous plants were raised. 'Czar' is a popular one, with long-stemmed, purple flowers that are good for cutting. 'Coeur d'Alsace' has rich rose-pink flowers.
Height 8cm (3in); **spread** 15cm (6in)
Cultivation Grow in a sheltered spot in dappled shade. Sweet violets prefer a moist, loamy soil. Plants are often grown in pots, making it easier to appreciate the scented flowers in late winter to early spring. Use a loam-based potting mix, and ensure plants do not overheat and dry out in summer. Propagate by division after flowering, or detach rooted runners.
Hardiness Fully hardy/Z5
Related plants Parma violets require more care than sweet violets and need winter protection in a cold frame or sheltered position. They will reward the grower with exquisitely scented, double flowers. *V.* 'Marie-Louise' has white-centred, mauve flowers, with occasional red streaks. *V.* 'Conte di Brazza' (syn. 'Swanley White') has soft creamy flowers.

Other collectors' plants
• *Dianthus* spp. (laced pinks) (AGM)
• *Hyacinthus orientalis* (hyacinth)

practicalities
All gardens require some level of care and attention. Cottage gardens, in particular, are not low-maintenance. Although densely planted beds and borders leave little room for weeds, some mediation is required to hold back the most vigorous plants. A productive garden also needs more care than most ornamental ones.

ABOVE: *Cutting out old stems will encourage new vigorous growth.*

TOP RIGHT: *Ensure that you remove all the roots of perennial weeds so that they cannot regrow.*

TOP FAR RIGHT: *Hoe on a dry, sunny day – this means that weeds will have a reduced chance of re-establishing.*

BOTTOM RIGHT: *Seedlings and cuttings require a gentle watering technique.*

MIDDLE: *Automatic watering devices deliver water to your plants based on the dryness of the soil – this cone and watering tube are connected to a small water container.*

FAR RIGHT: *Water plants thoroughly to encourage deep rooting, rather than little and often.*

OPPOSITE: *It is wise to group pot plants close to your access pathway and within easy reach of an outside tap.*

Weeding

Perennial weeds must be thoroughly removed when clearing the ground, as they are difficult to control when growing among your plants. If necessary, they can be gradually weakened by regularly removing the tops. Annual weeds can be pulled or hoed off as they appear (keep your hoe sharp). Try not to allow weeds to set seed. Some weeds, such as ragwort (*Senecio jacobaea*), are toxic to grazing animals. Try to prevent weeds germinating by using deep mulches over any bare soil.

Watering techniques

Good watering techniques will avoid wasting this precious natural resource. Water thoroughly, preferably in the morning or evening when temperatures are lower to reduce levels of evaporation. Mulching the soil surface with organic mulches, such as composted bark or well-rotted garden compost, minimizes

evaporation, but the soil should be moist before mulching or rain may not reach the plant roots. If water is in short supply, concentrate on watering new plantings and crops with a high water requirement such as tomatoes and lettuces. Investing in a water butt will enable you to collect rainwater from the roof of your home. Always have a lid for a water butt to prevent debris entering, and make sure that it is childproof.

Plants in containers require more watering than those in the open ground. Grouping pots together can create a damper microclimate and reduces the distance you have to cover with watering cans. Plastic pots retain water better than terracotta and can be used inside terracotta ones if you prefer the traditional look. Hanging baskets tend to dry out particularly quickly as they are exposed to wind. Lining them with old compost bags will reduce evaporation.

RIGHT: *Work base dressings of fertilizers around the root area of any shrubs that are in need of a boost.*

FAR RIGHT: *Removing old flowerheads from pelargoniums reduces the risk of them becoming mouldy and promotes new growth.*

RIGHT: *Hard pruning of these white-stemmed brambles will encourage new growth and a display of strong stems.*

FAR RIGHT: *Pruning side shoots back on apple trees in summer reduces the vigour of foliage and provides extra support for the fruit.*

RIGHT: *Here dead and damaged growth is removed from broom (Cytisus) to prevent disease.*

Deadheading

This is the removal of flowerheads from a plant as they fade so that the plant does not set seed. It is usually recommended in order to enable the plant to concentrate its energies on producing more flowers. Particularly useful with roses and sweet peas (*Lathyrus odoratus*), the technique does not work for all plants. Poppies (*Papaver*), for example, do not produce more flowers after deadheading. Do not deadhead if the seedpods or fruits are required for ornamental effect, as is the case with honesty (*Lunaria*), for instance.

Avoid deadheading plants if you want to save seeds, but choose the parent plants based on their overall health.

Feeding

Additional feeding should not be necessary for most plants, but particularly hungry crops such as tomatoes and cabbages, as well as plants growing in containers or grow bags, benefit from regular doses of fertilizer. These can be applied as a base dressing before planting or given in liquid or solid form throughout the growing season. Organic fertilizers are less likely to cause contamination problems if they leach into waterways. Always follow the manufacturer's directions when using chemical products. Applying organic mulches such as well-rotted animal manures to beds and borders is a traditional way of improving soil fertility.

Pruning techniques

From time to time, the gardener must intervene to ensure that no one plant takes more than its fair share of space. Many plants can be kept to a compact size in cultivation by pruning or confining root growth in a container. Always prune to a node (the small swelling on the stem where a bud or leaf emerges), so that stubs are not left which may attract disease.

Many overgrown shrubs and climbers that have become a tangled mass of woody stems can be cut back ruthlessly if they are healthy, but check first: some species will simply die if treated this way. For more routine pruning, cut back any crossing or congested shoots to an outward-facing bud or to the base. Remove any weak, spindly stems and create an open, evenly branched framework. Most deciduous shrubs are pruned straight after flowering. Plants such as hydrangeas, penstemons and fuchsias are usually pruned in the spring, so that the old shoots and flowers can provide frost protection through the winter.

Many conifers and Mediterranean shrubs, such as lavender and rosemary, will not regrow if they are cut back too hard into mature woody growth. If in doubt, just prune lightly and assess whether further cutting is required later. Shrubs such as dogwoods, willows and ornamental brambles can be cut down to ground level and will then produce vigorous new shoots and foliage for the coming season.

Pests and diseases

The rich mixture of plants in a cottage garden makes them less susceptible to pests and diseases, although problems do occur. Insects and other invertebrates are usually the most damaging, and some cause indirect damage to plants by spreading viral or fungal diseases.

There are various solutions to combat these problems. Use a jet water spray to shoot off aphids. Beer traps are an effective way to remove slugs and snails, or deter them by using copper tape around pots. For fruit and vegetables, use row covers made from horticultural fleece to protect crops from flying insects, and practise crop rotation to avoid soil-borne pests and diseases.

Pick off and burn any infected plant material, rather than placing it on the compost heap. Minor infestations can often be dealt with using the gardener's fingers or boot. Growing cultivars of plants that have resistance to disease will also reduce the need for chemicals. Encourage beneficial predators by having an insect border, including fennel and wild carrot for ladybirds, pollen- and nectar-rich flowers for lacewings and tall plants for spiders.

Pond maintenance

If ponds are kept clear of fallen leaves, and plants are thinned out regularly, they should only need a major clean every few years to remove decaying organic matter. Clean smaller ponds every four or five years; large ponds may be left for 10 years.

LEFT: *Rose black spot (Diplocarpon rosae) is a common fungal disease that will reduce a plant's vigour.*

Use a net to remove leaves and debris from the pond and periodically remove blanketweed (*Spirogyra*) by winding it around a bamboo cane or lifting it with a garden rake.

The formation of green algae is common in sunny weather and will be exacerbated by excess nutrients from fish faeces and rotting plant material. Using water plants such as *Nymphaea* or shrubs at the pondside to shade the water helps. There are also chemical treatments or ultra-violet sterilization techniques available but it is one treatment is unlikely to be totally effective.

Safety considerations

Accidents involving garden machinery such as lawnmowers, and lifting and falling injuries are common. If you are working with machinery, wear appropriate protective clothing. If children regularly use the garden, never leave them unattended near a pond and consider installing a safety grille. Check that the surfaces around the pond, particularly decking, are kept free from algal growth to reduce the chances of slipping.

Many plants are toxic, causing skin reactions when touched or poisoning when ingested. Children should be taught not to put anything in their mouth, unless they know it to be safe. The use of chemicals in the garden is another key hazard, particularly where children are concerned, so ensure the safe storage of chemicals and follow the manufacturer's instructions precisely.

TOP FAR LEFT: *Chickens in the garden help to reduce many pests such as these sawfly larvae – if left they will defoliate vulnerable plants.*

TOP LEFT: *If ponds are kept clear of fallen leaves and plants are thinned out regularly, as shown here, then they will only need a major clean out every few years.*

BOTTOM FAR LEFT: *Small children should have constant adult supervision when they are near water.*

BOTTOM LEFT: *Cover the tops of plant stakes with cane toppers or plant pots so that they cannot damage eyes.*

seasonal tasks
The rhythm of seasonal jobs in the cottage garden has changed little since medieval times, and many gardeners enjoy the familiar routines hailed by each season. However, you needn't be anxious about which jobs should be done when – gardens are forgiving places and there is always next year.

SPRING TASKS

In the flower garden

- Prune roses before new growth starts.
- Sow hardy annuals outside.
- Sow half-hardy and tender plants in a propagator or on a sunny windowsill.
- Cut back any herbaceous plants left over winter for their seedheads.
- Cut back any straggly evergreen shrubs to encourage new growth from the base.
- Lift and divide established herbaceous perennials.
- Tie in the new shoots of climbing plants to prevent them being damaged in windy weather.
- Mulch borders with well-rotted manure or garden compost.
- Plant up hanging baskets and window boxes.
- Plant out half-hardy plants, such as dahlias, after the last predicted frost.

In the fruit and vegetable garden

- Sow seeds of hardy vegetables outside.
- Hoe regularly to keep on top of weeds in the vegetable garden.
- Germinate tender vegetables such as tomatoes and aubergines (eggplants) on a windowsill or other warm space.
- Use cloches or cold frames to protect young seedlings from adverse weather.
- Protect young plants from slugs as the weather starts to warm up.
- Protect the blossom of early flowering fruit, such as peaches, apricots and nectarines, from frost with a layer of horticultural fleece.
- Plant out strawberry runners in new beds or pots.
- Spring-clean the chicken house, giving it a thorough scrub, and check for signs of parasites lurking in gaps and under the roof, spraying if necessary.
- Groom goats as they shed their winter coat and make sure that their worming programme is up-to-date.
- Sterilize spare beehives with a blow-torch in preparation for the new season.

ABOVE FROM LEFT: *Cleaning the chicken coop; a peony shelter; and straw mulch.*

SUMMER TASKS

In the flower garden

- Prune spring-flowering shrubs once they have finished flowering.
- Cut down herbaceous perennials as they finish flowering to encourage a second flush of flowers.
- Take semi-ripe cuttings of many shrubs and climbers.
- Water newly planted trees thoroughly in dry weather.
- Deadhead annual plants to prolong the display.
- Prune the current year's growth of wisteria back to the first five leaves to restrict growth and promote better flowering.
- Stake tall-growing perennials such as delphiniums and some dahlias.
- Lift and divide primroses and polyanthus after they have finished flowering, replanting in a shady spot.
- Watch out for red lily beetles on fritillaries and lilies, squashing them if seen.
- Keep birdbaths topped up with fresh water during hot weather.

In the fruit and vegetable garden

- Harvest early potatoes and other crops such as peas and summer spinach.
- Plant out calabrese (Italian sprouting broccoli), Brussels sprouts and other brassicas.
- Thin out plums and apples to allow remaining fruits to expand properly.
- Protect fruit crops from birds with horticultural fleece or netting.
- Check the leaves of brassicas for the eggs of white butterflies, squashing them if seen.
- Gather and dry herbs for winter use.
- Summer-prune fruit trees to encourage fruit buds next year.
- Evict broody hens from the nest box unless you want them to hatch eggs.
- Make sure that goats have plenty of fresh water, especially when nursing kids.
- Add extra honey supers (a box placed above the brood chamber) to hives to prevent the bees swarming.

  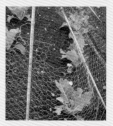

ABOVE FROM LEFT: *Maran hen; herb collection; and wire netting crop protection.*

ABOVE: *Narcissus and grape hyacinth*

ABOVE: *Summer flower basket*

ABOVE: *Apple 'Katja'*

ABOVE: *Winter aconite* (Eranthis hyemalis)

AUTUMN TASKS

In the flower garden

- Collect seeds from favourite plants for use next year.
- Take cuttings of pelargoniums and other tender perennials.
- Plant out spring bedding plants such as wallflowers (*Erysimum cheiri*), double daisies (*Bellis perennis*) and forget-me-nots (*Myosotis*).
- Bring tender plants under cover before the first frosts.
- Plant spring bulbs for a colourful display next year.
- Lift and divide herbaceous perennials if not done in spring.
- Make leaf mould by stacking fallen leaves in a wire netting cage or black bags.
- Sow sweet peas (*Lathyrus odoratus*) in a sunny, sheltered site.
- Replace summer-flowering plants with those of winter and spring interest.
- After the first frost, lift dahlias, cut back the top growth and store tubers over winter in buckets of sand.

In the fruit and vegetable garden

- Plant hardy lettuces such as 'Winter Density' in grow bags or pots.
- Tie grease bands around apple tree trunks to catch female winter moths.
- Sow broad beans such as 'Aquadulce Claudia' for a springtime crop.
- Prune out fruited canes of blackberry and hybrid berry bushes.
- Grow green manure crops such as Italian ryegrass on bare soil in the vegetable garden, to be dug into the soil in spring.
- Finish picking outdoor tomatoes and either bring individual fruits inside to ripen or hang the vines up in a potting shed or garage.
- After harvesting autumn-fruiting raspberries, cut canes down to the ground.
- Chickens will go into moult and will stop laying eggs until new feathers have grown. Ensure that they have a good nutritious diet to replace protein losses.
- For female goats to kid in spring, you need to find a male for autumn mating.
- When the honey crop has been removed from hives, check that the bees have sufficient stores for their own use.

WINTER TASKS

In the flower garden

- Plant out bare-rooted trees, shrubs and hedging, as long as the ground is not waterlogged or frozen.
- Cut deciduous hedges before the birds start building their nests.
- Make bird and bat boxes in order to encourage wildlife to visit the garden.
- Take hardwood cuttings of deciduous shrubs.
- Check and repair wooden fences, trellis and posts.
- Brush snow from evergreen shrubs to prevent the branches snapping under the weight.
- Order summer-flowering bulbs such as *Galtonia* and *Tigridia* for spring planting.
- Cut willow stems to make yourself a willow arbour.
- Check plant labels and replace any that are brittle or faded.
- Sit in front of a fire, looking through the seed catalogues to make your selection of what to grow next year.

In the fruit and vegetable garden

- Winter-prune fruit trees to encourage vigorous new growth.
- Clear old crops from vegetable beds and spread a layer of garden compost to improve the soil.
- Apply a light dressing of lime to the brassica bed if your soil is acid (but not at the same time as manure).
- Prune grapevines (*Vitis vinifera*), using the prunings as hardwood cuttings.
- Check stored fruit regularly, removing any that show signs of rot.
- Clean and store bamboo canes in the shed so that they are ready for use.
- Cut hazel or sweet chestnut bean poles for use in the spring.
- Check the security of the chicken run to make sure foxes cannot enter.
- Ensure all livestock has ice-free water available in frosty conditions.
- Make sure that beehives are waterproof and able to resist strong winds.

ABOVE FROM LEFT: *Spring bulbs; pelargonium cuttings; and making leaf mould.*

ABOVE FROM LEFT: *Nest box; bird feeders in the snow; and storing pears.*

useful addresses

SUPPLIERS

AUSTRALIA
Redpath's Beekeeping Supplies
193 Como Parade East, Parkdale,
Victoria 3195; T: (03) 9587 5950;
www.redpaths.com.au

Yarrabee Garden and Iris
71 Lanacoon Rd, Mt Compass,
SA 5210
T: (61) 438 817 577;
www.yarrabeegardenandiris.net
Plants and seeds

CANADA
The Cottage Gardener
4199 Gilmore Rd, RR 1 Newtonville,
Ontario L0A 1J0
www.cottagegardener.com
Plants and seeds

Nature's Garden Seed Company
7361 Bell McKinnon Road, Duncan,
BC, V9L 6A9; T: (877) 302-7333;
www.naturesgardenseed.com

EUROPE
Cayeux Iris
La Carcaudière, Route de Coullons
45500 Poilly-Lez-Gien,
France; T: (238) 670 508
www.iris-cayeux.com

Pivoines Rivière
La Plaine, 26400 Crest, France
www.pivoinesriviere.com;
T: (0)4 75 25 44 85
Plants and seeds

UK
Agroforestry Research Trust
46 Hunters Moon, Dartington, Totnes,
Devon TQ9 6JT; T: 01803 840776
www.agroforestry.co.uk
Plants and seeds

Binny Plants
Binny Estate, Ecclesmachan, West
Lothian, Scotland EH52 6NL
T: 01506 858931
www.binnyplants.com

Chiltern Seeds
Crowmarsh Battle Barns, 114 Preston
Crowmarsh, Wallingford, OX10 6SL;
T: 01491 824675
www.chilternseeds.co.uk

David Austin Roses
Bowling Green Lane, Albrighton,
Wolverhampton WV7 3HB;
T: 0800 111 4699
www.davidaustinroses.co.uk

Flyte so Fancy
Anne and Phillip Weymouth,
The Cottage, Pulham, Dorchester,
Dorset DT2 7DX
T: 01300 345229
www.flytesofancy.co.uk
Poultry supplies

Forsham Cottage Arks
Goreside Farm, Ashford, TN26 1JU;
T: 01233 820229
Chicken sheds

C W Groves and Son
The Nurseries, West Bay Road,
Bridport, Dorset DT6 4BA T: 01308
422654; www.grovesnurseries.co.uk
Plants and seeds

The Place for Plants
East Bergholt Place, Suffolk CO7 6UP
T: 01206 299224;
www.placeforplants.co.uk
Plants and seeds

Smallholder Feeds
Norfolk Mill, Shipdham, Thetford,
Norfolk IP25 7SD T: 01362 822900
www.smallholderfeed.co.uk
Chicken food

Woottens of Wenhaston
Blackheath, Wenhaston, Halesworth,
Suffolk IP19 9HD T: 01502 478258;
www.woottensplants.com
Plants and seeds

USA
The Beez Neez Apiary Supply
403A Maple Ave., Snohomish, WA
98290 T: 360-568-2191;
www.beezneezapiary.com
Beekeeping

Mt. Tahoma Nursery
28111 112th Ave E., Graham, WA 98338
www.backyardgardener.com/mttahoma

The Strawberry Store
107 Wellingston Wa7, Middleton,
DE 19709
T: (302) 379-4778
www.thestrawberrystore.com

NEW ZEALAND
Clifton Homestead Nursery
2 R.D. Clinton, South Otago; T: (03)
4157-212; www.hellebores.co.nz

Hereweka Garden Retreat
10 Hoopers Inlet Rd, RD2, Dunedin
9077, T: 63-478 0165;
www.hereweka.co.nz

GARDENS TO VISIT

Ballyrobert Cottage Garden
154 Ballyrobert Rd, Ballyclare, Co.
Antrim, BT39 9RT, N. Ireland, T: 02893
440101; www.ballyrobertcottage.com

Barnsdale Gardens
The Avenue, Exton, Oakham,
Rutland LE15 8AH
T: 01572 813 200;
www.barnsdalegardens.co.uk

Bide-a-wee Cottage Gardens
Stanton, nr. Netherwitton, Morpeth,
Northumberland NE65 8PR T: 01670
772238; www.bideawee.co.uk

Cobble Hey Farm
off Hobbs Lane, Claughton on Brock,
Garstang, Lancashire PR3 0QN T: 01995
602643; www.cobblehey.com

East Lambrook Manor Gardens
East Lambrook, South Petherton,
Somerset TA13 5HH T: 01460 240
328; www.eastlambrook.com

Stone House Cottage Garden
Church Lane, Kidderminster, DY10
4BG T: 07817 921146
www.shcg.co.uk

Burrow Farm Gardens
Dalwood, Axminster, Devon
EX13 7ET T: 01404 831285;
www.burrowfarmgardens.co.uk

Claude Monet's Garden
Fondation Claude Monet, 84 rue
Claude Monet, 27620 Giverny, France
T: 2 32 51 28 21; giverny.org

Daniel Stowe Botanical Gardens
6500 South New Hope Road,
Belmont, NC 28012, USA
T: (704) 825-4490; www.dsbg.org

The Garden House
Buckland Monachorum, Yelverton,
Devon PL20 7LQ T: 01822 854769;
www.thegardenhouse.org.uk

Sissinghurst Castle Garden
Sissinghurst, Cranbrook, Kent
TN17 2AB T: 01580 710701;
www.nationaltrust.org.uk/sissinghurst-
castle-garden

Wyken Hall Gardens
Wyken Hall, Stanton, Bury St Edmunds,
Suffolk IP31 2DW T: 01359 250287;
www.wykenvineyards.co.uk

SOCIETIES

American Dairy Goat Association
167 West Main Street, PO Box 865,
Spindale, NC 28160 USA T: (828)
286-3801; www.adga.org

**Australian Miniature Goat
Association**
T: (64) 428 430 294
amga@amga.com.au
www.amga.com.au

The British Beekeepers Association
The National Agricultural Centre,
Stoneleigh Park, Warwickshire
CV8 2LG T: 0300 020 6649;
www.bbka.org.uk

The Cottage Garden Society
'Brandon', Ravenshall, Betley, Cheshire
CW3 9BH T: 01270 820 940;
www.thecottagegardensociety.org.uk

Garden Organic
Ryton Gardens, Wolston Lane,
Coventry, Warwickshire CV8 3LG
T: 02476 303517;
www.gardenorganic.org.uk

Hardy Plant Society
15 Basepoint Business Centre,
Crab Apple Way, Evesham WR11 1GP
T: 01386 710317;
www.hardy-plant.org.uk

Seed Savers Exchange
3094 North Winn Rd, Decorah, Iowa
52101 United States T: (563) 382-
5990; www.seedsavers.org

Seeds of Diversity Canada
112 Dupont St West, Waterloo
ON On2L 2X6 T: (226) 600-7782
mail@seeds.ca
www.seeds.ca

index

plant hardiness zones

Plant entries in the directory of this book have been given hardiness descriptions and zone numbers. Hardiness definitions are as follows:

Frost tender

A plant needing heated greenhouse protection through the winter in the local area. May be damaged by temperatures below 5°C (41°F).

Half hardy

A plant which cannot be grown outside during the colder months in the local area and needs greenhouse protection through the winter. Can withstand temperatures down to 0°C (32°F).

Frost hardy

A plant which survives through milder winters in the local area, with additional protection. Withstands temperatures down to −5°C (23°F).

Fully hardy

A plant which, when planted outside, survives reliably through the winter in the local area. Can withstand temperatures down to −15°C (5°F).

There is widespread use of the zone number system to express the hardiness of many plant species and cultivars. This system, shown here, was developed by the Agricultural Research Service of the US Department of Agriculture.

It uses 11 zones, based on the average annual minimum temperature in a particular geographical zone.

Each plant's zone rating indicates the coldest zone in which a correctly planted subject can survive the winter. Where hardiness is borderline, the first number shows the marginal zone and the second the safer zone.

This is not a hard and fast system, but a rough indicator, as many factors other than temperature play a part where hardiness is concerned. These factors include altitude, wind exposure, water proximity, soil type, the presence of snow or shade, night temperature, and the amount of water received by a plant. Such factors can alter a plant's hardiness by as much as two zones. The presence of long-term snow cover in the winter especially can allow plants to survive in colder zones.

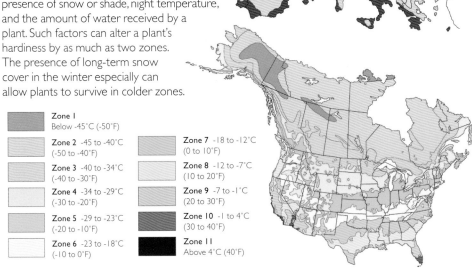

Zone 1 Below −45°C (−50°F)
Zone 2 −45 to −40°C (−50 to −40°F)
Zone 3 −40 to −34°C (−40 to −30°F)
Zone 4 −34 to −29°C (−30 to −20°F)
Zone 5 −29 to −23°C (−20 to −10°F)
Zone 6 −23 to −18°C (−10 to 0°F)
Zone 7 −18 to −12°C (0 to 10°F)
Zone 8 −12 to −7°C (10 to 20°F)
Zone 9 −7 to −1°C (20 to 30°F)
Zone 10 −1 to 4°C (30 to 40°F)
Zone 11 Above 4°C (40°F)

acknowledgements

With grateful thanks to the companies and individuals who allowed us to take photographs: Anne Hathaway's Cottage, Stratford-Upon-Avon (The Shakespeare Birthplace Trust); Cathryn Draper, Amber Green Farmhouse, Kent; Amwell Cottage, Hertfordshire; Avenue Cottage, Hampshire; Copyhold Hollow Bed & Breakfast, West Sussex; Judith Hitching, Gowers Close, Oxfordshire; Mrs Cox, Ivy Nook; Margaret & Jon Penny, Leechpool Cottage, West Sussex; Margery Jones, Rose Cottage, Bedfordshire; Rosefern Cottage, Gloucestershire; Julie Wise, Rustling End Cottage, Hertfordshire; and C. Apperley, Stonecroft, Gloucestershire.

The publishers would also like to thank the following agencies and individuals for permission to reproduce their images: **Alamy:** p12br The Art Gallery Collection; p14b Mike Kipling Photography; p15r Country Collection/Homer Sykes; p18m HOBBS; p18b Ron Niebrugge; p19tl Daniel Dempster Photography; p19tr imagebroker; p19b David Robertson; p109m Veljo Runnel; p109r Ernie Janes; **Corbis Images:** p20br & p21r Hulton-Deutsch Collection; **The Bridgeman Art Library:** p10bl Osterreichische Nationalbibliothek, Vienna, Austria/Alinari; p10br Musée des Beaux-Arts, Lille, France/Giraudon; p11 Josef Mensing Gallery, Hamm-Rhynem, Germany; p12bl Rafael Valls Gallery, London; p13 Private Collection; p14m Peter Nahum, The Leicester Galleries, London; p17b Private Collection/Mallett Gallery, London; **Gap Photos:** p25 Michael King; p37, p78bl, p97, p111bl Elke Borkowski; p31r Neil Holmes; p75, p111t J. S. Sira; p78r, p133t Jonathan Buckley; p92 Friedrich Strauss; p94t, p132b Howard Rice; p100bl Michael King; p103t Leigh Clapp; p108bl Suzie Gibbons; p108r Jason Smalley; p110bl Zara Napier; p118bl Marcus Harpur; p118bm Dave Bevan; p125t Eric Crichton; p134r Martin Hughes-Jones; p135b Olive & David Mason; p137t Michael Howes; p138t Richard Bloom; p139tm Geoff Kidd; p143l FhF Greenmedia,; p143b, p149l John Glover; **Getty Images:** p17t Apic; **Felicity Forster:** p30, p55br, p80tl; **Garden Picture Library:** p106br Francesca Yorke; **istock:** p119b; **Lucy Doncaster:** p106bl; **Photolibrary:** p109bl.

Author's acknowledgments

Thanks to Jill Bennett of the Cottage Garden Society and to the many other members who were full of useful suggestions and allowed us to photograph their gardens.

Thank you to photographer Howard Rice who is always a delight to work with and has an endless supply of creative ideas, and at Anness to Emma Clegg — I hope the love of snowdrops is growing within you.

And with special thanks to my sons Ashley and Jonathan who make every day in our garden a sunny day.